Practical Action Publishing Ltd
27a Albert Street, Rugby, CV21 2SG, Warwickshire, UK
www.practicalactionpublishing.org

First published by Oxfam International in April 2009.
Reprinted by Practical Action Publishing

© Oxfam International 2009

Paperback ISBN: 9780855985271
PDF ISBN: 9780855988029

A catalogue record for this publication is available from the British Library.

Front cover image: Haiti: members of the Civil Protection Committee of Borgne take part in a training exercise to learn how to save lives in a flood. The smaller-scale disasters that regularly hit rural areas of Haiti are increasing, and can be devastating for local communities.
Abbie Trayler-Smith / Oxfam GB Back cover image: A porter loads supplies onto an Oxfam helicopter, bound for the mountainous northern regions of Pakistan affected by an earthquake (2005).Carlo Heathcote / Oxfam

Summary

There is a crisis destroying the livelihoods of 25 million coffee producers around the world. The price of coffee has fallen by almost 50 per cent in the past three years to a 30-year low. Long-term prospects are grim. Developing-country coffee farmers, mostly poor smallholders, now sell their coffee beans for much less than they cost to produce – only 60 per cent of production costs in Viet Nam's Dak Lak Province, for example. Farmers sell at a heavy loss while branded coffee sells at a hefty profit. The coffee crisis has become a development disaster whose impacts will be felt for a long time.

Families dependent on the money generated by coffee are pulling their children, especially girls, out of school. They can no longer afford basic medicines, and are cutting back on food. Beyond farming families, coffee traders are going out of business. National economies are suffering and some banks are collapsing. Government funds are being squeezed dry, putting pressure on health and education and forcing governments further into debt.

The scale of the solution needs to be commensurate with the scale of the crisis. A Coffee Rescue Plan, which brings together all the major players in the coffee trade, is needed to make the coffee market benefit the poor as well as the rich. This is about more than coffee. It is a key element in the global challenge to make trade fair.

The coffee market is failing. It is failing producers on small family farms for whom coffee used to make money. It is failing local exporters and entrepreneurs who are going to the wall in the face of fierce international competition. And it is failing governments that had encouraged coffee production to increase export earnings.

Ten years ago producer-country exports captured one-third of the value of the coffee market. Today, they capture less than ten per cent. Over the last five years the value of coffee exports has fallen by US$4bn; compare this with total debt repayments by Honduras, Viet Nam, and Ethiopia in 1999 and 2000 of US$4.7bn.

The coffee market will also, arguably, end up failing the giant coffee-processing companies, at present so adept at turning green beans into greenbacks. The big four coffee roasters, Kraft, Nestlé, Procter & Gamble, and Sara Lee, each have coffee brands worth US$1bn or more in annual sales. Together with German giant Tchibo, they buy almost half the world's coffee beans each year. Profit margins are high – Nestlé has made an estimated 26 per cent profit margin on instant coffee. Sara Lee's coffee profits are estimated to be nearly 17 per cent – a very high figure compared with other food and drink brands. If everyone in the supply chain were benefiting this would not matter. As it is, with farmers getting a price that is below the costs of production, the companies' booming business is being paid for by some of the poorest people in the world.

Paying prices as low as they can go – whatever the consequences for farmers – is a dangerous business strategy in the long term. And even in the short term it does not help the business interests of the producers of instant coffee. It is particularly risky given that these companies depend on the goodwill of consumers. The rise of Fair Trade sales in recent years has demonstrated that consumers care about the misery of those who produce the goods they buy.

The coffee industry is in the process of a radical and, for many, extremely painful overhaul. It has been transformed from a managed market, in which governments played an active role both nationally and internationally, to a free-market system, in which anyone can participate and in which the market itself sets the coffee price. Recently this has brought very cheap raw material prices for the giant coffee companies.

At the same time, Viet Nam has made a dramatic entry into the market and Brazil has increased its already substantial production. The result is that more coffee is being produced and more lower quality coffee traded, leading to a cataclysmic price fall for farmers. Eight per cent more coffee is currently being produced than consumed. In the meantime coffee companies have been slow to comply with what one of them identified as being their core responsibility within the current crisis: the generation of demand for coffee. The current growth rate of 1-1.5 per cent per year in demand is easily outstripped by a more than two per cent increase in supply.

Despite the stagnant consumer market, the coffee companies are laughing all the way to the bank. In the free market their global reach gives them unprecedented options. Today's standardised coffee blends may be a mix of coffees from as many as 20 different coffee types. Sophisticated risk management and hedging allows the companies, at the click of a computer mouse, to buy from the lowest-cost producer to mix these blends.

At the other end of the value chain the market does not feel so free. Without roads or transport to local markets, without technical back-up, credit, or information about prices, the vast majority of farmers are at the mercy of itinerant traders offering a 'take it or leave it' price. Their obvious move out of coffee and into something else is fraught with problems. It requires money that they don't have and alternative crops that offer better prospects. For a farmer to turn her back on the four years spent waiting for coffee trees to start bearing fruit is a highly risky strategy.

The coffee-market failure is also, in part, a result of stunning policy failure by international institutions. The World Bank and the IMF have encouraged poor countries to liberalise trade and pursue export-led growth in their areas of 'comparative advantage'. The problem for many poor countries is that the advantage can be very slim indeed – as the flood of coffee and other primary agricultural commodities onto global markets shows. These countries are stuck selling raw materials that fail, utterly, to capture the value added by the time the product hits the supermarket shelves.

Even within the free coffee market, these institutions can be charged with dereliction of duty. Where was the sound economic advice to developing countries on overall global commodity trends, and their likely impact on prices? What urgent steps are donor governments taking to ensure that efforts to create a more manageable debt burden for the poorest countries are not undermined by commodity shocks?

Until now, rich consumer countries and the huge companies based in them have responded to the crisis with inexcusable complacency. In the face of human misery, there have been many words yet little action. Existing market-based solutions – Fair Trade and the development of specialty coffees – are important, but only for some farmers. They can help poverty reduction and the environment. However, a systemic, not a niche solution, is needed.

The challenge is to make the coffee market work for all. The failures of previous efforts at intervention in the market must be understood and lessons learned. But so too must the lessons of the moment. The low coffee price creates a buyers' market, leaving some of the poorest and most powerless people in the world to negotiate in an open market with some of the richest and most powerful. The result, unsurprisingly, is that the rich get richer and the poor get poorer. Active participation by all players in the coffee trade is needed to reverse this situation.

The next year is critical. Coffee-producing governments have agreed a plan that aims to reduce supply by improving the quality of coffee traded. This will only work if it is backed by the companies and by rich countries and is complemented by measures to address long-term rural underdevelopment.

Oxfam is calling for a Coffee Rescue Plan to make the coffee market work for the poor as well as the rich. The plan needs to bring together the major players in coffee to overcome the current crisis and create a more stable market

Within one year the Rescue Plan, under the auspices of the International Coffee Organisation, should result in:

1. Roaster companies paying farmers a decent price (above their costs of production) so that they can send their children to school, afford medicines, and have enough food.

2. Increasing the price to farmers by reducing supply and stocks of coffee on the market through:

   - Roaster companies trading only in coffee that meets basic quality standards as proposed by the International Coffee Organisation (ICO).

   - The destruction of at least five million bags of coffee stocks, funded by rich-country governments and roaster companies.

3. The creation of a fund to help poor farmers shift to alternative livelihoods, making them less reliant on coffee.

4. Roaster companies committing to increase the amount of coffee they buy under Fair Trade conditions to two per cent of their volumes.

The Rescue Plan should be a pilot for a longer-term Commodity Management Initiative to improve prices and provide alternative livelihoods for farmers. The outcomes should include:

1. Producer and consumer country governments establishing mechanisms to correct the imbalance in supply and demand to ensure reasonable prices to producers. Farmers should be adequately represented in such schemes.

2. Co-operation between producer governments to stop more commodities entering the market than can be sold.

3. Support for producer countries to capture more of the value in these commodities.

4. Financed incentives to reduce small farmers' overwhelming dependence on agricultural commodities.

5. Companies paying a decent price for all commodities, including coffee.

1

The crisis in coffee

Peris Mwihaki pruning her coffee bushes after the harvest in Kenya's Central Province. In recent years her coffee cherries have brought her no more than 2-3% of the final selling price of Kenyan AA coffee on supermarket shelves in the North. "Payments don't reach us here in the hills," Peris explained. "The farm is just as hard work as it ever was, but we're getting nothing in return."

1. The crisis in coffee

There is a crisis affecting 25 million coffee producers around the world. The price of coffee has fallen to a 30-year low and long-term prospects are grim. Developing-country coffee farmers, the majority of whom are poor smallholders, now sell their coffee beans for much less than they cost to produce. The coffee crisis is becoming a development disaster whose impact will be felt for a long time.

Families dependent on money generated by coffee are pulling their children, particularly girls, out of school, can no longer afford basic medicines, and are cutting back on food. Beyond farming families, national economies are suffering. Coffee traders are going out of business, some banks are in trouble, and governments that rely on the export revenues that coffee generates are faced with dramatically declining budgets for education and health programmes and little money for debt repayment.

If globalisation is to work for the poor – if trade is to work for the poor – then the coffee market cannot fail the poor in the way it is doing at present. It does not have to be this way.

Crisis, what crisis?

Glance down any major shopping street in the rich world and you will be reassured that the coffee industry is thriving. Coffee bars offering the youthful camaraderie of the global TV series *Friends* have sprung up in prime real-estate locations. Bookshops and department stores house in-store cafés emitting the smell of fresh coffee and the murmur of tired shoppers. Railway station coffee booths offer a quick shot of caffeine for commuters well-versed in the respective merits of espressos, café lattes, and cappuccinos.

In the boardrooms of the world's four biggest coffee companies, known as roasters – Kraft Foods, Nestlé, Procter & Gamble, and Sara Lee – business is also humming. Between them, these four companies control the major coffee brands: Maxwell House, Nescafé, Folgers, and Douwe Egberts. Kraft – itself controlled by Philip Morris, the tobacco company – made profits of over US$1bn on sales of beverages, cereals, and desserts in 2001. Nestlé's instant coffee – 3,900 cups of which are drunk every second – makes such healthy profits that one investment analyst described it as the commercial equivalent of heaven.[1]

So lucrative is the industry that it comes as a shock to many to realise that producing this apparently golden bean leaves millions of farmers in deep poverty. One coffee farmer in Uganda summed up the desperation of many of the farmers interviewed by Oxfam:

'I'd like you to tell people in your place that the drink they are enjoying is now the cause of all our problems. We [grow] the crop with our sweat and sell it for nothing.'
– Lawrence Seguya, Mpigi District, Uganda. February 2002[2]

The challenge facing the world's coffee market is a sharp illustration of the challenges involving many commodities on which developing countries rely heavily. Finding a solution to this crisis is a test of whether globalisation – and the market that it creates – can be made to work for poor people.

When coffee turns from boom to bust....

For farmers throughout the developing world, coffee used to hold out hope for a better future.

Coffee is one of the few internationally traded commodities that is still mainly produced not on large plantations but on smallholdings farmed by peasant households. Seventy per cent of the world's coffee is grown on farms of less than ten hectares – and of this, the vast majority is grown on family plots of between one and five hectares. Even in countries that do have large plantations, such as Brazil, India, and Kenya, there are many smallholder producers as well.

Smallholder farmers used to reap good benefits from their crop. They could feed their families well, send their children to school and afford decent housing. In the Kilimanjaro region of Tanzania, for instance, cash from coffee meant high literacy rates and above-average nutritional levels.[3] In Colombia, cash from coffee financed schools, infrastructure, and training for farmers. Coffee-producing regions have been less prone to the political violence affecting other areas of that country – a factor that has been attributed in part to the relative prosperity of coffee farmers.

Coffee is grown in the wide tropical and sub-tropical belt around the Equator, including in some of the countries facing the most severe development challenges in the world (figure 1). There are two main varieties: robusta and arabica. Robusta – as its name indicates – is a hardy plant. It is used widely for soluble coffee and in the stronger roasts. The better-quality arabica – with its milder flavour – is typically grown at higher altitudes. It is harder to grow and more susceptible to disease but it commands a higher price. It is sold in specialty coffee markets, as well as being used in soluble coffee blends for its flavour.

Figure 1: World coffee production, 2001

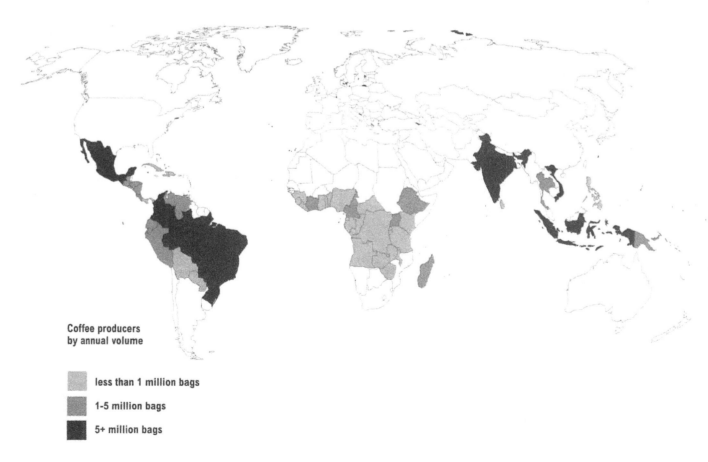

Coffee producers
by annual volume

less than 1 million bags

1-5 million bags

5+ million bags

The economies of some of the poorest countries in the world are highly dependent on trade in coffee. Dependency is particularly high in some African countries. In Uganda, the livelihoods of roughly one-quarter of the population are in some way dependent on coffee sales. In Ethiopia, coffee accounts for over 50 per cent of export revenues, while in Burundi the figure is almost 80 per cent (figure 2). In Guatemala, more than seven per cent of the population is dependent on coffee for its livelihood; in neighbouring Honduras, nearly 10 per cent.[4] In Nicaragua, the second poorest country in Central America, coffee accounts for seven per cent of national income.[5]

Even where national economies are not dependent on coffee, regions and communities sometimes are. In Mexico, coffee is still of great importance, especially to the 280,000 indigenous farmers living mostly in the poorer states of Oaxaca, Chiapas, Veracruz and Puebla. In Brazil, although coffee provides less than five per cent of total foreign exchange earnings, it provides a livelihood for between 230,000 and 300,000 farmers and employs a further three million people directly in the coffee industry.[6] In India, the coffee industry employs three million workers.[7]

Figure 2.   Heavy dependence on coffee for cash
Coffee exports as a percentage of total exports (2000)

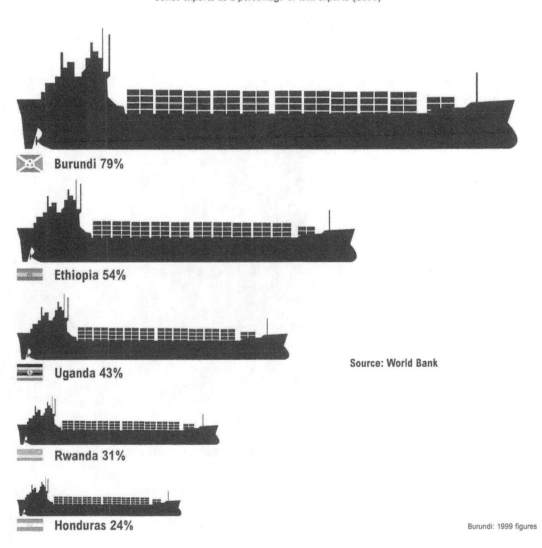

Burundi 79%

Ethiopia 54%

Uganda 43%

Source: World Bank

Rwanda 31%

Honduras 24%

Burundi: 1999 figures

The devastation of coffee communities and countries

The price paid to farmers for their coffee – for both robusta and arabica – has fallen appallingly low. In 1997 it started on a steep decline, hitting a 30-year low at the end of 2001 and still hovering around that level in June 2002. Taking inflation into account, the 'real' price of coffee beans has fallen dramatically lower: it is now just 25 per cent of its level in 1960, meaning that the money that farmers make from coffee can only buy one-quarter of what it could 40 years ago (figure 3). This is probably the lowest real price farmers have been paid for coffee in 100 years.

Landell Mills Consultants estimated that the coffee price at the end of 2001 did not cover the total costs of either robusta or arabica producers. In the case of robusta, the price did not even cover variable costs. I n Viet Nam, for instance, one of the lowest-cost producers in the world, Oxfam's research in Dak Lak province suggests that, at the beginning of 2002, the price farmers were receiving covered as little as 60 per cent of their production costs.[8]

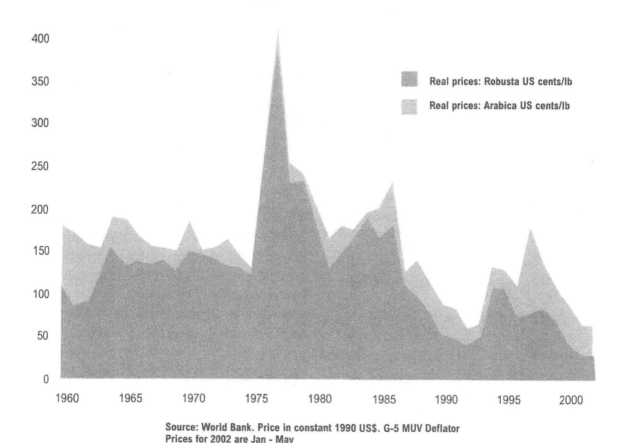

Figure 3. The dramatic fall in real prices for coffee
Arabica and robusta, US cents/lb

Real prices: Robusta US cents/lb

Real prices: Arabica US cents/lb

Source: World Bank. Price in constant 1990 US$. G-5 MUV Deflator
Prices for 2002 are Jan - May

These are terrible times for farmers, who are despairing at a coffee price that does not allow them to cover their families' most basic needs. Most have relied on the cash from their coffee for essential items, and typically have no savings to help them in hard times. Some are forced to sell off their land; others are leaving their homes and families in search of work elsewhere, which has a knock-on effect on entire communities.

'In some communities, we see that migration to Mexico is very big. In one community, about three or four months ago, about eight trucks came in and took away all the people who could work to Mexican fincas... they stayed there between four to six months. That means social disruption of the family is incredible,' says Jeronimo Bollen, from a Guatemala co-operative, Manos Campesinos.[9]

Desperate farmers in Mexico or Honduras dream of escaping to the US. In 2001, six coffee farmers from Veracruz trying their luck were found dead in the Arizona desert.[10]

According to Cesar Villanueva of the NGO Rainforest, *'The price crisis hits women very directly. The [male] head of the family often goes to work elsewhere, at least for part of the year, leaving the women and children to work the land. Usually this means children abandoning school.'* The workload of women has also increased in families used to buying in casual labour to help with the coffee harvest. Now that they can no longer afford to do so, women often take on the extra work.

Mohammed Ali Indris, an Ethiopian coffee farmer from Kafa province interviewed by Oxfam in March 2002, gave a graphic sense of how the price collapse had affected his family. He is 36 years old and his household of 12 includes the children of his deceased brother. Around five years ago, he estimates, he could make about $320 a year from the combined sale of coffee and corn. This year he expects around $60 for the coffee. The corn he would have sold has already been eaten by his family.

'Five to seven years ago, I was producing seven sacks of red cherry [unprocessed coffee] and this was enough to buy clothes, medicines, services and to solve so many problems. But now even if I sell four times as much, it is impossible to cover all my expenses. I had to sell my oxen to repay the loan I previously took out to buy fertilisers and improved seed for my corn, or face prison.

'Medical expenses are very high as this is a malaria-affected area. At least one member of my household has to go to hospital each year for treatment. It costs US$6 per treatment. We also need to buy teff [staple starch], salt, sugar, soap, kerosene for lighting. We have to pay for schooling. Earlier we could cover expenses, now we can't... Three of the children can't go to school because I can't afford the uniform. We have stopped buying teff and edible oil. We are eating mainly corn. The children's skin is getting dry and they are showing signs of malnutrition.' [11]

Families going hungry

According to the World Food Programme in March 2002 the coffee crisis, combined with the effects of a drought, had left 30,000 Hondurans suffering from hunger, with hundreds of children so malnourished that they needed to be hospitalised.[12] *'Hunger has become commonplace in parts of Central America, particularly in north eastern Guatemala, where drought has seriously hit basic grains production and the World Food Programme has been forced to mount a series of emergency programmes,'* reports Oxford Analytica.[13]

In January 2002 the EU and USAID warned of increased poverty and food security issues for coffee farmers in Ethiopia, saying that farmers were selling their assets and cutting down on food. Farmers interviewed by Oxfam in Peru say they have had to cut back heavily on food. In Viet Nam's Dak Lak province, the income derived by the worst-off farmers, dependent solely on coffee, is now categorised as 'pre-starvation'.

Hunger is particularly acute in households that have opted to dedicate a higher proportion of land to coffee than to other subsistence crops. The decisions about this balance can be a source of conflict between women who are responsible for feeding their families, and men keen to earn a higher cash income.

Children forced out of school
In many of the interviews Oxfam has conducted, in Viet Nam, East Africa, and Peru, farmers cited the coffee price as a problem in ensuring a decent education for their children.

In Uganda, where such a large proportion of the population depends in part on coffee, the crisis is hitting the ability of families to send their children to school.

Bruno Selugo (aged 17) and his brother Michael (15), who live in Mpigi District, Uganda, have both had to drop out of school because they cannot afford the fees. *'I can't be successful if I don't go to school,'* says Bruno. *'I will just be left here, growing a little food. I have been sent home again and again from secondary school ... They just send you away if you don't have the fees ...This is the main coffee season. Everyone used to go back to school with the money from coffee, but now the money is not there. The price is so low people are not even picking coffee... I wish the people who use our coffee could give us a better market. All I want is to go to school.'*

Patrick Kayanja, head teacher at Bruno's school, explains, *'The number of students is very low. Much as we try to reduce the fees, the parents cannot pay. They always took cash from selling coffee but now it is gone. There was a time, between 1995 and 1997, when we had 500 students. Three years ago we had 250. Last year we started with 140 and ended with 54. This year we cannot go beyond 120, the way I see the situation with farmers.'* [14]

Worsening health care
The combination of falling coffee incomes, plus rising health demands, is having devastating impacts on health care. In Ethiopia, where coffee is the major export and 700,000 households depend on it for their livelihoods and millions more for part of their income,[15] the fall in coffee export earnings poses

serious challenges to the country's ability to deal with the HIV/AIDS crisis. The UN Agency on HIV/AIDS estimates that over three million adult Ethiopians (five per cent of the population) are now infected with the virus. The Ministry of Health has projected that treatment for HIV/AIDS alone will account for over 30 per cent of total health expenditure by 2014.

The burden of the disease not only has the potential to make extraordinary and unrealisable claims on the government's health budget, which in part must be funded by coffee revenues. Like other developing countries in which state health provision is extremely limited, individuals and their families have to pay for health and medicine costs out of their own pockets.

The economic costs of HIV/AIDS are high: low productivity caused by sickness, the burden of finding money to pay for medical care and drugs, and funeral expenses. These costs are already reaching several times the average household income of Ethiopia's rural poor. For those families reliant on diminishing returns from coffee, the situation is intolerable. Women are particularly badly affected, both because of the added responsibilities arising from ill-health in the family and because they tend to go without when families have to make choices about who receives treatment.

Destitute seasonal workers and labourers
Seasonal workers and labourers are among the poorest and most vulnerable participants in the coffee trade. They work for a wage on the small and medium-sized farms (10-50 hectares) and big plantations (more than 50 hectares), which produce 30 per cent of the world's coffee. Away from home they are unable to supplement food intake by crops grown on their own land and can suddenly find themselves out of work.

Although some producer countries maintain decent labour standards in the coffee sector this is not always the case: many coffee workers are unable to unionise to negotiate wages. Even where labour legislation exists, too often it is ignored and workers' rights overridden. Women are often paid less than men for the same work (up to 30 per cent less in Honduras) and the use of child labour is common. In Kenya, for example, 30 per cent of coffee pickers are under fifteen.[16]

In Central America some 400,000 temporary and 200,000 permanent coffee workers have recently lost their jobs, according to the World Bank.[17] In Guatemala, many of the seasonal workers are indigenous Indians who leave their homes for the harvest in the hope of earning enough money to buy staples such as cooking oil, salt, and clothing for the rest of the year. Even prior to the fall in coffee prices the working and living conditions of these labourers was often deplorable. They are typically housed in large barns or bunk-houses with no privacy, lacking basic requirements such as clean water and adequate sanitary arrangements.

The crisis has driven many to desperate measures. In the coffee-growing regions of Guatemala there have been widespread land invasions by unemployed casual labourers, after small growers laid off up to 75 per cent of their pickers in January 2002.[18] In Karnataka, which produces a large proportion of India's coffee, there has been a 20 per cent fall in the number of plantation workers over the last two years.[19]

Growing attractions of growing drugs

The coffee crisis has had some unexpected impacts on development. In Peru, Colombia, and Bolivia the conditions required for growing coffee are very similar to those in which coca – the raw material for cocaine – is grown. For decades, Andean countries have been under considerable pressure, particularly from the US Drug Enforcement Agency (DEA), to play their part in the 'war against drugs' by participating in programmes to destroy the coca that is used in cocaine production. The fall in the coffee price has created serious threats to the programmes designed to replace coca with other crops.

'People are definitely replacing coffee with coca. In the Sauce area it is somewhat hidden, since CORAH [the drug eradication agency] is still quite active in the area. But CORAH can't keep pace with it. Coffee is a waste of time from a strictly economic point of view...Everyone has some coca, despite the fact that there is a price to be paid. Everyone is aware of this. It brings violence – assaults and rape. It also brings prostitution and gang warfare.'
– Ing. Guillermo Lopez[20] Sauce, Peru

Financial crises for national economies

The slump in the coffee price has severe impacts far beyond the immediate farming communities: it has become a development crisis for the predominantly poor countries that grow the crop. The drying up of coffee cash in the local economy is one of the main reasons behind the collapse of several banks. In Central America, the crisis has been said to be having the *'impact of another [hurricane] Mitch'* in terms of income losses: these countries have seen revenue from coffee exports fall 44 per cent in one year alone, from $1.7bn in 1999/2000 to $938m in 2000/01. Forecasts for 2001/02 are grim: a further fall of 25 per cent.[21]

In sub-Saharan Africa, the same story prevails. Ethiopia's export revenue from coffee fell 42 per cent, from $257m to $149m, in just one year.[22] In Uganda, where roughly one-quarter of the population depends on coffee in some way, coffee exports for the eight months to June 2002 remained at almost the same volume as the year before but earnings dropped by almost 30 per cent.[23]

There is a double whammy here for producer countries: the price of their exports tends to decline over time, but the price of their imports, often manufactured goods, does not fall as fast, leading to a deterioration in their terms of trade. Figure 4 shows that a coffee farmer would have to sell more than twice as many coffee beans now as in 1980 to buy a Swiss Army Knife

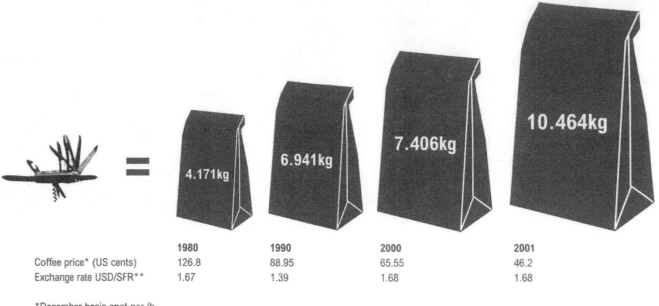

Figure 4: How much coffee does it take to buy a Swiss Army Knife?

	1980	**1990**	**2000**	**2001**
Coffee price* (US cents)	126.8	88.95	65.55	46.2
Exchange rate USD/SFR**	1.67	1.39	1.68	1.68

*December basis spot per lb
** Annual average

Source: Gerster Consulting

Worse, the cost of debt is fixed in US dollars but the dollar value of coffee exports is falling steadily, making it increasingly unaffordable to keep up debt repayments. The poorest countries benefit from debt relief initiatives (including the Heavily Indebted Poor Countries initiative). But the slump in export revenues undermines these efforts to put poor countries' finances on an even keel.

Ethiopia's exports from coffee slumped in one year from $257m to $149m.[24] To put this into perspective, in 2002, the country's projected savings on servicing its debt will be $58m (from HIPC and other debt relief).[25] The Minister of Agriculture in Nicaragua, Jose Augusto Navarro, singled out the burdens of debt repayment as another immense challenge on top of all the other misery that the coffee price is causing his country.[26]

Tragically, far from creating a healthy agricultural sector and yielding up much-needed foreign exchange, coffee has ended up requiring governments to take emergency measures to support their coffee farmers. Colombia has allocated $72m to finance a domestic price subsidy for growers.[27] In 2001 Costa Rica had to make US$73m available in interest-free emergency credit to farmers.[28] In Thailand the government is aiming to purchase over half of the 2001/02 crop at a fixed rate which, though still lower than the costs of production, is significantly higher than the price farmers would otherwise be paid.[29]

2

The roots of the crisis

George Sakwa holding arabica coffee cherries harvested from his family's smallholding on the slopes of Mount Elgon in Uganda. In 2001 George and his wife Topista sold 1.5 acres of their farm because the returns from selling coffee could no longer meet their children's secondary school fees.

2. The roots of the crisis

The coffee market is facing a crisis of slumping prices and falling quality. For farmers the loss of quality means lower prices, even for arabica varieties that once earned a high premium – this is bad for farmers, bad for coffee drinkers and ultimately bad for the roasters. Behind this devastating situation lie four major factors:

a. market restructuring: from managed to flooded

b. power imbalances in the market: penniless farmers, profiting roasters

c. new roaster technologies and techniques: driving down quality

d. no alternatives: the failures of rural development.

Market restructuring: from managed to flooded

The market is severely oversupplied: the volume of coffee produced to be traded far outstrips demand. Production in 2001/02 is estimated at 115 million bags[30] – each one weighing 60kg – compared with consumption of 105-106 million bags[31] (figure 5). Supply has been growing at more than two per cent each year, outstripping growth in demand of 1-1.5 per cent.[32] This year-on-year excess supply has built up stocks now estimated at over 40 million bags.[33] Even if supply were to come into line with demand any time soon – and some expect this by 2003/04 – the presence of these stocks would still keep the coffee price at a depressed level.

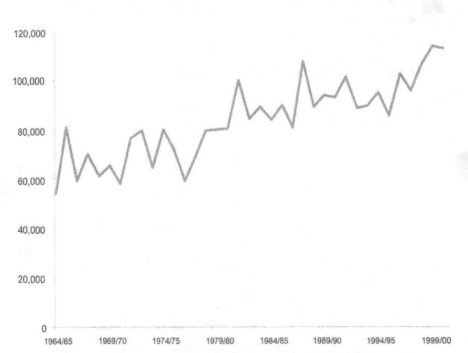

Figure 5: World coffee production 1964-2001 ('000s bags)

Source: ICO

Three reasons explain how supply and demand have got so far out of line: the end of the managed market in 1989, major new entrants into the market, and lagging demand in traditional Western markets.

The breakdown of the managed market

Over the past 15 years the coffee market has changed radically. Until 1989, coffee – like most commodities – was traded in a managed market, regulated by the International Coffee Agreement (ICA). Governments in both producing and consuming nations sought to agree pre-determined supply levels by setting export quotas for producing countries. The aim was to keep the price of coffee relatively high and relatively stable, within a price band or 'corset' ranging from $1.20/lb to $1.40/lb. To prevent oversupply, countries had to agree not to exceed their 'fair' share of coffee exports. If, however, prices rose above the ceiling level, producers were permitted to exceed their quotas to meet the surge in demand.

Disagreement between members led to the effective breakdown of the Agreement in 1989. Opposition from the US, which subsequently left as a member, was a major factor. The Agreement survives, administered by the International Coffee Organisation (ICO), but it has lost its power to regulate the supply of coffee through quotas and the price corset. Prices for coffee are determined on the two big futures markets based in London and New York, with each market trading particular varieties and grades of coffee. The London market is the benchmark for robusta coffee, the New York for arabica. The price of coffee is influenced by the huge number of contracts for coffee that are traded, which far exceeds the physical amount of coffee that changes hands.

From the perspective of producer countries, the Agreement brought a golden era of good and stable prices, compared with the present development disaster. As figure 6 shows, from 1975 to 1989, though prices fluctuated significantly, they remained relatively high and rarely fell below the ICA price floor of $1.20/lb. In sharp comparison, once the Agreement broke down and the price corset ended in 1989, prices dropped dramatically and – apart from two sharp price spikes in 1995 and 1997 caused by frost ruining the Brazilian crop – prices have fallen very low, even below the average cost of production.

Figure 6: Monthly New York Coffee futures (spot month)

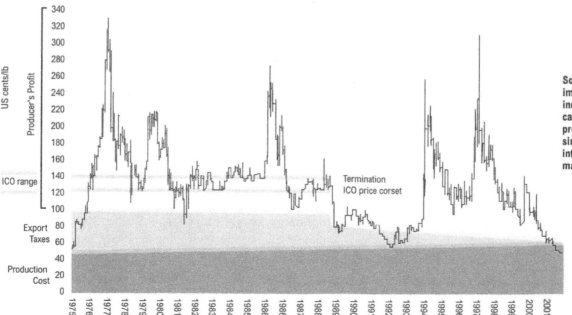

Source: Volcafe. It is important to note that individual farmers did not capture the full 'producer's profit' as indicated here, since much was absorbed by intermediaries and inefficient marketing chains.

Critics point to many reasons for the Agreement breaking down. There was cumbersome political horse-trading in the struggle to capture larger quotas, and it was difficult for new producers trying to enter the market. Despite agreed quotas, additional volumes leaked out to countries outside the Agreement, undermining its intended prices and undermining trust. Some in the industry believe that the price corset laid the ground for overproduction because the coffee price was artificially set too high – but others argue that the current glut probably owes its origins more to the price hikes of 1994/95 and 1997 than to the high coffee prices of the 1980s.

Proposals to revive the Agreement are impeded by the apparent lack of political will to make it work. Consumer nations show no willingness to participate at present and producer nations may not be willing or able to abide by their own rules. In the absence of consumer country support, producer countries did attempt to limit their own exports, but the initiative collapsed in 2001. The lack of will to revive this approach to managing markets through quotas does not mean that other approaches could not work, especially those that would operate through market mechanisms. The ICO has developed just such an approach: a scheme to reduce the amount of coffee traded on grounds of quality. But this initiative will only work if rich countries and coffee roasters back it.

Enter the giants: Brazil and Viet Nam

Brazil and Viet Nam have reshaped the world's coffee supply. Ten years ago, Viet Nam was barely a statistical blip in the coffee world, producing just 1.5m bags. Its agricultural economy was opened to the world market during the 1990s, with the government providing subsidies to encourage farmers to grow coffee. By 2000, it had become the second largest producer in the world with 15m bags to its name, largely produced on small farm-holdings.

Brazil, on the other hand, is not a newcomer: it has long been the world's largest producer, but production has recently been boosted by changes in how and where coffee is grown. Increased mechanisation, intense production methods and a geographical shift away from the traditional, frost-prone growing areas have all increased yields. The forthcoming and widely anticipated bumper crop from Brazil, offsetting declines in exports elsewhere, will mean a continuing imbalance in supply.[34]

In addition to dramatically increased supply, the impact for traditional coffee-producing countries is serious: they now face competition from unprecedented levels of productivity. *'To give you an idea of the difference, in some areas of Guatemala, it could take over 1000 people working one day each to fill the equivalent of one container of 275 bags, each bag weighing 69kg. In the Brazilian cerrado, you need five people and a mechanical harvester for two or three days to fill a container. One drives, and the others pick. How can Central American family farms compete against that?'* asks Patrick Installe, Managing Director of Efico, a green coffee trader.[35]

What were the triggers for the jump in world coffee production and the resulting oversupply? Freak price hikes in 1994/5 and 1997, due to frosts in Brazil, certainly encouraged countries, and their farmers, into the market. But other factors were also at play in producer countries. National policies, new technologies, and currency movements were also important influences.

Lagging demand

The US, Germany, France and Japan between them consume half of world coffee exports.[36]

While coffee production has grown rapidly, demand for coffee in the developed world has seen sluggish growth although newer markets, such as Eastern Europe, show greater promise. The big coffee companies spend millions of dollars on advertising each year, but they have failed to stop rich consumers turning to alternative drinks. Figure 7 shows just how badly coffee consumption has done compared with the growth in soft drinks in the US, the world's largest consumer market. This is not a worldwide picture, however. Nestlé, whose share of the US market is relatively small, states that it has boosted consumption of Nescafé by 40 per cent over the last ten years.

Figure 7: US coffee consumption – a nation goes soft
US coffee consumption vs. soft drinks consumption in gallons per capita

23 Gallons — 1970

53 Gallons — 2000

36 Gallons — 1970

17 Gallons — 2000

Source: US Department of Agriculture/Davenport & Company

Figures for 2000 are forecasts
Figures for coffee based on 3-year moving average

The combination of oversupply, increased production and lagging demand has created a severely imbalanced market which cannot simply be left to its own devices if supply and demand are to be brought back into line. The human toll of such an approach is unacceptable: the market makes no suggestions as to what farming families are supposed to live on while waiting several years for the market to 'clear'.

Power imbalances in the market: penniless farmers, profiting roasters

While this crisis has been going on, coffee has been a bonanza market for the transnational roaster companies. Far from getting a fair share of its profitability, producer countries have collectively been receiving a smaller and smaller share of the market's value.

• Ten years ago, producer countries earned $10bn [37] from a coffee market worth around $30bn. A decade later, they receive less than $6bn of export earnings from a market that has more than doubled in size. That's a drop in their share from over 30 per cent of the market to under 10 per cent.

• Today coffee farmers receive one per cent or less of the price of a cup of coffee sold in a coffee bar. They receive roughly six per cent of the value of a pack of coffee sold in supermarkets and grocery stores.

A glance at figure 8 shows how marginal the actual coffee beans have become to the whole business of selling the beverage to consumers. In 1984, green bean costs constituted 64 per cent of the US retail price. By 2001 the raw material price as a proportion of the final retail value had fallen to 18 per cent. [38] Some markets may be giving consumers a better deal than others but, in all of them, the importance of coffee beans to the final retail price has fallen.

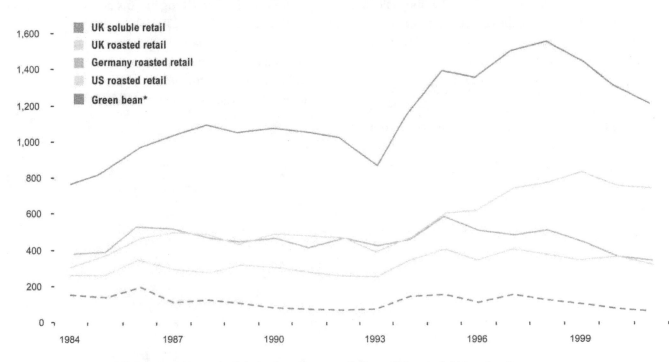

Figure 8: Coffee price comparison nominal prices 1984-2001 (US cents/lb)

Legend:
- UK soluble retail
- UK roasted retail
- Germany roasted retail
- US roasted retail
- Green bean*

*ICO nominal price composite index. Green beans = coffee beans that are traded internationally and processed into instant or roast/ground coffee.

Source: ICO. Soluble coffee is not comparable to roast and ground: a consumer can get more cups of coffee from one pound of soluble than he or she can from one pound of roast and ground.

There is a vast imbalance of power in the global coffee supply chain. Farmers face a whole series of obstacles, starting with the very low international price for coffee. But some farmers Oxfam spoke with also complained of having to accept the price offered by the trader and of having very little, if any, power to negotiate. If farmers process their coffee (removing the outer layer of the coffee cherry) they can demonstrate the quality, or 'grade', of their beans and so negotiate a better price. But if their coffee is sold in its cherry form, they are not rewarded for its as yet unknown quality.

In Peru, even when the coffee is sold as semi-processed 'parchment', farmers can still be short-changed: *'We see that the coffee is dry, but the buyers say: give us a discount... I don't know what grade it is, but I think they are taking advantage of us because they know we have to sell to them,'* says Carmela Rodriguez, from Sauce, Peru.[39] Co-operatives often give farmers an alternative to the harsh terms of traders: farmers reported that they sold their better-quality coffee to the co-operatives where they were rewarded with premiums, but still found the traders useful as ready buyers of their lower-quality coffee.

Even though traders squeeze extra margins for themselves out of farmers, the real margins in the market are made, after export, by the roaster companies.

In sharp contrast with the current losses, or at best tiny margins, made by farmers and exporters in developing countries, the roaster companies in the US and Europe are making extraordinary profits on their retail coffee business.

Oxfam interviewed many players in the supply chain in Uganda to trace the rising price of coffee beans as they made their journey from the farmer's trees to the jars sitting on supermarket shelves in the UK – and found that, in this case, the farmer got just 2.5 per cent of the retail price of the coffee. In the US, the figure would be 4.5 per cent of the retail price (see section *Where do all the profits go?*). Beyond the story in Uganda, Oxfam commissioned a consultant to construct an indicative value chain to try to assess what percentage on average of the end value farmers were getting in different countries around the world – and found that farmers of the cheapest type of coffee, doing no processing to their coffee cherries, are getting just 6.5 per cent of the final retail value, like for like. This value chain uses official price data, where available, weighted to take into account different market shares.[40] Even this figure is probably an overestimate, since official data on prices to producers may overstate what farmers actually get.

Where do all the profits go?
Tracing the value chain...

'Go to the Sheraton Hotel in Kampala and you'll pay 60 US cents for a cup of coffee. In Europe you can pay twice as much. We don't understand what's happening. The farmer doesn't understand. How can the farmer grow a kilogram of kiboko [local unprocessed coffee] for eight US cents, and see a spoonful sold for 60 US cents? Are the roasters cheating? Are they making superhuman profits? The only way that all Ugandans can stay in Uganda and not disturb European countries is to have a better price for our crops.' [a]

These are the words of a coffee buyer for Volcafe in Uganda. He may be an employee of a giant transnational trading house, but he speaks here as a local man asking a fundamental question: where do all the profits go? Oxfam traced the costs that go into the price of coffee through interviewing people who are part of the value chain in Uganda, showing how value is added to coffee as it moves from the farmer, through the various stages of processing and distribution, until it finally lands up on the supermarket shelf. It reveals how the tiny profit margins in that value chain suddenly widen once the coffee reaches the hands of roasters and retailers.

The coffee farmer receives 14 US cents per kilo for his green beans, assuming he does no processing. These beans pass through various traders before arriving at the roaster factory at a price of $1.64 per kilo. If these beans were to end up in a soluble coffee sold on supermarket shelves in the UK, an average price per kilo would be $26.40. Adjusting for loss of weight along the way, between farm gate and shopper's trolley the price would have inflated by more than 7000 per cent. An equivalent journey into a pack of roast and ground coffee sold in the US would involve a price rise of nearly 4000 per cent. [b]

Kituntu region lies in Uganda's Mpigi District, about 100km south-west of Kampala, just a few miles south of the equator and at an altitude of about 1,200 metres. It is typical of the coffee-growing area to the north and west of Lake Victoria, which produces most of Uganda's robusta crop.

The farmer: not even covering costs

Peter and Salome Kafuluzi live on their farm in Kituntu with 13 of their children and grandchildren. They have lived and planted coffee in Kituntu since 1945. Interviewed by Oxfam in February 2002, Peter said the last time he sold coffee, the price he got was the lowest he'd ever seen. A whole kilogram of the sun-dried coffee cherry, known locally as *kiboko*, was fetching 6 or 7 US cents. *'I remember when kiboko sold for 69 US cents/kg. We fed well, we slept well without worries. We could support our families. For me, I'd need to see a price of at least 34 US cents/kg. Even at 29 US cents/kg, we can't look after the land.'*

Salome says: *'We're broke. We're not happy. We're failing in everything. We can't buy essentials. We can't have meat, fish, rice, just sweet potatoes, beans and matoke... We can't send the children to school.'*

The *kiboko* needs to be milled to remove the outer casing of the cherry, yielding about half of its weight as the green coffee bean that is traded worldwide. It makes more financial sense for farmers to get their coffee milled themselves, and many do. Peter sold some of his coffee at the mill and got a better price for it. But some farmers don't have enough coffee to justify the cost of the pick-up truck and are too far away to take their coffee to the mill by bicycle. These farmers have to take the lower price offered by the local middlemen for their unprocessed cherries.

The miller: struggling to survive

Mary Goreti has run the Jalamba coffee mill near Kituntu for ten years. The mill employs ten people, but the slump in the coffee price is taking its toll on business. *'The profit margins are so small now, and the [cost of the] electricity we use is so high, we can't manage to make ends meet. We have so few people bringing kiboko. Some farmers are just keeping it at home because prices are so low. If the coffee price stays low, the business will fail. You can't open a factory to process ten bags,'* she says.

The exporter: barely covering costs

From Jalamba, the coffee is trucked 100km to Kampala and sold to an exporter. One such exporter is Hannington Karuhanga, managing director of Ugacof. Hannington's office has large windows that give views over the factory and the rows of stacked shipping containers. The computer screen flickers and he rattles off percentages and prices at the click of a mouse. For him too, the sums don't add up. He says that exporters are *'very happy now to make a margin of $10 a tonne net (1 US cent per kg).'* Hannington sorts, grades, cleans, and bags up the coffee and trucks it to either Mombasa or Dar es Salaam. The price he receives for his coffee is essentially the export price (Free On Board, or FOB, price). He says it barely covers his costs. Prices have fallen so low, he says. *'Some of these grades [different qualities of coffee] we have are not worth transporting. It would be cheaper to destroy them.'*

The retailer: sky-high prices

Jumping to the other end of the supply chain, retailers in the UK sell one kilogram of soluble coffee on average for $26.40 – an enormous leap in prices. Of course this price includes the many costs of processing, packaging, distributing, and marketing the coffee – as well as the roasters' and retailers' profits. Ugandan coffee used to be used frequently in UK coffees but is now used less – so we cannot be sure that the final retail price includes coffee from this particular origin. But the Uganda value chain stands as a useful indicator of a competitive and fairly efficient market in this type of coffee. The best price Peter and Salome Kafuluzi could have got for their coffee, selling it hulled at the mill, represented roughly 2.5 per cent of the final retail price in 2001, once adjustments had been made for the weight lost in processing. [c]

[a] Oxfam background research in Uganda

[b] The multiple for adjusting the loss of weight is 2.6 times for soluble and 1.19 times for roast and ground. The base figure is the worst of the two prices the farmer was paid.

[c] Adjusting for loss of weight

Who is making profits in the coffee market chain?

All prices in US$/kg   November 2001 – February 2002

Prices traded

Costs and margins

**Farmer sells kiboko to middleman
(equivalent price 1kg of green beans)** $0.14

0.05   Local middleman's margin
0.05   Costs of transport to local mill, cost of milling, miller's margin
0.02   Cost of bagging and transport to Kampala

**Price of green coffee (Fair Average Quality)
arriving at the exporter's in Kampala** $0.26

0.09   Exporter's costs: processing, discarding off-grades, taxes and exporter's margin
0.10   Bagging, transport, insurance to Indian Ocean port

FOB price for Standard Grade robusta $0.45

0.07 Cost of freight, insurance

CIF price  $0.52

0.11   Importer's costs: landing charges, delivery to
roaster's facility, importer's margin

**Price delivered to factory
(adjusted for weight loss for soluble: x2.6)** $1.64

The FOB price is for a standard Uganda grade 15 robusta. Returns for exporters are dragged down by lower prices for lesser grades. The retail price is the September 2001 price for soluble in the UK, drawn from ICO statistics.

Retail price for average 1kg of soluble in the UK

$26.40

Roaster power: heavenly profits in the midst of crisis

There are a great many roasters around the world who buy green coffee beans and turn them into roast and ground or instant coffee for drinkers. But the four main roasters – Kraft, Nestlé, Procter & Gamble, and Sara Lee – are giants in the coffee world and shape its retail market. Their widely recognised brands include Maxwell House, Nescafé, Folgers, and Douwe Egberts. Procter & Gamble sells coffee in North America (figure 9), while the fifth biggest roaster, Tchibo, sells mainly in Germany.

Recently, coffee drinking in rich countries has undergone something of a transformation. Fancy coffee bars have mushroomed, egging consumers on to ever more exotic coffee tastes (white chocolate mocha anyone?). The specialty coffee sector has grown rapidly, now accounting for about 40 per cent of the value of US coffee market sales, according to one estimate.[41] But, in terms of volumes, it is the major roasters shifting millions of coffee bags that affect developing countries the most. Between them, the five companies mentioned above buy almost half of the world's supply of green coffee beans.

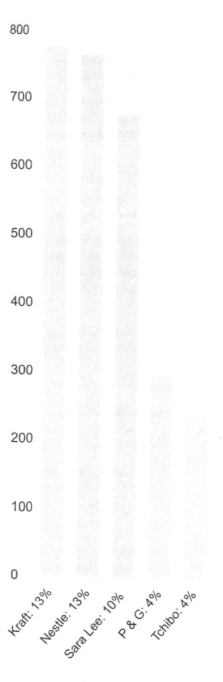

Figure 9: Top roasters – annual green coffee volume, 2000 ('000 metric tons)

Source: Volcafe

Exact profit figures for these companies are hard to pin down because their coffee business is often buried within larger food and drink subsidiaries and results are not disclosed publicly. Nonetheless, analysts' estimates explain why these companies are so addicted to their coffee highs.

Two years ago, an analyst report on Nestlé's soluble business concluded: *'Martin Luther used to wonder what people actually do in heaven. For most participants in the intensely competitive food manufacturing industry, contemplation of Nestlé's soluble coffee business must seem like the commercial equivalent of Luther's spiritual meditation.'*[42]

Referring to Nestlé's market share, size of sales and operating profit margins, the same author said: *'Nothing else in food and beverages is remotely as good'.* The report estimates that, on average, Nestlé makes 26p of profit for every £1 of instant coffee sold.[43] Another analyst believes that margins[44] for Nestlé's soluble business worldwide are higher, closer to 30 per cent. For Nestlé, the rich markets of the UK and Japan are particularly profitable.

Roast and ground coffee is less profitable than soluble, but the profits are still enviable. In 2002 Sara Lee, buffeted by competition in the US market, still managed a more than decent operating profit margin of nearly 17 per cent for its beverages unit,[45] which deals mostly in coffee.

A quick glance at profits made in other food and drink markets reveals just how mouth-watering these profit levels are. The Heineken beer group, for instance, managed a margin of around 12 per cent in 2001. Sara Lee's margins on its deli meats and sausage business were under 10 per cent in 2002;[46] its profits on breads and bakery were even lower, at 5.5 per cent. Danone's dairy and yoghurt business managed around 11 per cent in 2001. Coffee – and especially soluble coffee – is a cash cow by comparison.

How do these roaster companies manage to be so profitable while farmers are in such deep crisis? They gain from the volumes they buy, from the strength of their brands and products, from cost control, from their ability to mix and match blends and from the use of financial tools that give them even more buying flexibility.

• Brand power

The famous names of the leading brands command significant premiums over the actual cost of the products they sell. Companies spend millions each year to build their brand images: in the UK, for example, advertising expenditure on instant coffee brands was $65m in 1999, mainly on Nescafé, Kenco, and Douwe Egberts, according to Key Note research.[47] With distinct brands, roasters can distinguish their products through image and taste, so avoiding competing with each other on price alone.

Brand power also gives roasters serious negotiating clout with the retailers who stock their products. Just how much clout is the stuff of long, hard and secretive negotiations between roasters and retailers. The major retailers – the leading supermarkets – are very powerful themselves and have picked up on the profit potential of coffee by launching their own-brand labels.

In some markets, such as Germany and France, industry figures say that retailers are putting pressure on roasters to keep prices very low. But there is a limit to how much pressure the retailers can exert on the big four or five roasters: they know that shoppers expect to find classic brands on their shelves.

	KRAFT	**Nestlé**
Statements on Corporate Social Responsibility	Kraft Foods shares together with its consumers, customers and the coffee industry as a whole, the concern for the long-term sustainability of good quality coffee. This means we support ...A decent and improving standard of living for growers and producers of coffee and their families.[a]	A few years down the r... maximised short-term... questions. Among the... hunger in developing...
Views on the Crisis	The market will find its own solution because countries and producers will be driven out of the market. Our role is on the demand side – our role as Kraft is to increase consumption.[c] As the original producers of vital raw commodities for our quality products, farmers must be able to achieve an acceptable overall level of financial return in order to remain viable participants in the coffee sector on a long-term basis.[d]	Nestlé is concerned ab... receiving historically l... disturbing increase in... Nestlé is against low p... Nestlé's business. Wh... low prices inevitably l... negatively impact our...
Views on Control of Oversupply in the Coffee Market, including the ICO Quality Scheme	Our role in the coffee industry is to provide coffee products at reasonable prices that meet both the quality and values expectations of our consumers. The ICO quality initiative has been offered as one means of addressing the current price environment. Therefore, we are giving this program careful evaluation to fully understand its implications for our complex global business and its potential contribution to constructively addressing the current market situation.[f] It won't work. It never has because it is a voluntary scheme and because it is unclear what it is trying to do. We are fundamentally opposed to any scheme that intervenes on price.[g]	Nestlé fully supports t... as it pertains to the ex... Nestlé considers the I... to set up a price stabili... initiative requires the... importing countries. U... remains the only viabl... Nestlé supports any c... governmental agencie... helping the individual...
Actions Taken to Address the Crisis	Kraft has spent $500,000 on a quality improvement scheme in Peru. It claims that its efforts in conjunction with a local cooperative, Cocla, to introduce better quality standards has improved the overall price that Peru receives for its coffee. Kraft also supports quality improvement in Viet Nam, focused on the arabica producing area of Tan Lam in conjunction with Douwe Egberts, GTZ and the Tan Lam company.[f]	Nestlé has a number... small farmer. Mexico...
Price & Premiums Paid for Coffee [i]	Kraft pays a quality differential for a large proportion of the green coffees we purchase. The significant majority of our coffee is purchased from exporting companies in countries of origin. Therefore we cannot assess directly the magnitude of benefits that accrue to specific farmers. However, as a general matter we believe that producers of coffees for which we pay quality differentials receive higher prices than they would in the absence of these differential payments.[f]	About 13% of our cof... is paid for quality. Th... premium varies from... sure that this is the ca...

[a] Kraft Foods "Sustainability - an important issue in the brand orientated food industry" presented to Oxfam 23 April 2002

[b] Peter Brabeck-Letmathe, CEO Nestlé, 30 November 1999 "The Search for Trust".

[c] Interview with Oxfam 23 April 2002

[d] Letter to Senator Sam Farr 7 March 2002

[e] Low coffee prices Causes and Potential Solutions – Presentation to CSR Europe 12 July 2002

[f] Kraft letter to Oxfam 26 June 2002

[g] Interview with Oxfa...

[h] Nestlé letter to Oxfa...

[i] No company was pr... prices paid for coffe...

oad, we are going to be asked not only if we have
shareholder value, but also some other, more difficult
m will certainly be: What have you done to help fight
countries?[b]

out the plight of those coffee farmers who are presently
w prices for their coffee crop. This situation results in a
poverty and suffering for themselves and their families. [e]

rices as they are not only bad for farmers, but also bad for
le in the short term they reduce the cost of raw materials,
ad to high prices and it is these wide swings which
business.[e]

he ICO Quality Improvement Scheme and its application
ort of green coffee from producing countries.[h]

ternational Coffee Organisation (ICO) as the best platform
ation mechanism, since the success of this kind of
ommitment of the governments of both producing and
nless an entirely new system is to be created, the ICO
forum. [h]

rdinated effort between governments, industry, intra-
and NGOs to eliminate the boom to bust cycle and
offee farmer.[e]

projects in place to help improve the situation of the
one example of this. [h]

is bought through direct purchasing, where a premium
mechanism of ensuring that the farmer benefits from the
untry to country, but we have controls in place to make
[h]

Sales $33,875m [i]
Profit $4,884m [ii]
**Beverages, desserts and
cereals section $1,192m** [iii]
(FY end 31 December 2001)

Major brands
Philadelphia, Tang, Jello,
Oscar Mayer, Oreo, Milka,
Lifesavers

Coffee brands
Maxwell House, Jacobs,
Café Hag, Carte Noire,
Gervalia Kaffe, Nabob

**Products bought by 99.6%
of all US households.**

Sales $50,415m [iv]
Profit $5,487m [v]
Beverages section $2,535m [vi]
(FY end 31 December 2001)

Major brands
Nestlé, Nescafé, Nestea,
Maggo, Buitoni and Friskies

Coffee brands
Nescafé, Gold Blend

**3,900 cups of Nescafé are dru
every second in more than 12
countries across the globe.**

23 April 2002
26 June 2002
ared to disclose the average

[i] Operating Revenues
[ii] Operating income (consolidated statement of earnings)
[iii] North American Operating Co. income
[iv] Sales to Customers

[v] Trading profit
[vi] Results
[vi] Net sales
[viii] Operating income

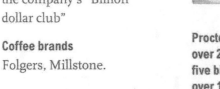

P&G

Sales $39,244m [vii]
Profit $4,736m [viii]
Food and beverages section $547m [ix]
(FY end 30 June 2001)

Major brands
Pringles, Iams, Pampers, Always & Ariel. 11 brands in the company's "Billion dollar club"

Coffee brands
Folgers, Millstone.

Procter & Gamble markets over 250 brands to nearly five billion consumers in over 140 countries

---

Sara Lee

Sales $17,747m [x]
Profit $2,037m [xi]
Beverages section $485m [xii]
(FY end 30 June 2001)

Major brands
Playtex, Wonderbra, Hanes, Sara Lee (cakes)

Coffee brands
Douwe Egberts, Uniao, Pilao, Superior Coffee, Maison de Cafe

$20bn in annual revenue from sales in 180 countries

Statements on Corporate Social Responsibility

P&G has alwa
value of "doin
management
environmenta
involvement i

Views on the Crisis

No-one in co

We recognize
current situat
help address
situation and
long-term sys

Views on Control of Oversupply in the Coffee Market, including the ICO Quality Scheme

We support t
adequate, su
consumers,
such as the C
coffees. [i]

P&G suppor
P&G is not p
because it is

Actions Taken to Address the Crisis

As a compan

Local - Contr
and Venezue

Business Un
to help small

Corporate - F
Conservancy

Price & Premiums Paid for Coffee

P&G buys a s
with offices i
Department
exporters hel
chain."

Before tax earnings

Net sales

Operating Income

Operating Income

[i] P&G on Corpo
www.pg.com/a
[i] Interview with

's conducted its business with integrity and a strong P&G core
; the right thing." We have long been leaders in human resource
employee compensation and benefits, -workplace safety,
management of our operations, ethical business practices and
t the communities where we have operations.[i]

Sara Lee's objective is to utilize the corporation's purchasing power to influence those from whom the corporation procures products and services to: embrace high standards of ethical behavior, comply with all applicable laws and regulations, treat their employees fairly, and with dignity and respect, so as to promote their welfare and improve their quality of life, and be socially responsible citizens in the countries and communities in which they operate.

---

e can deny the crisis.[k]

he social problems many coffee-growing families face given the
on of global over-production and low prices. P&G is committed to
ie underlying social and economic issues which contribute to this
/e want to work with reputable organizations that can help provide
emic solutions.[l]

Sara Lee and the coffee industry at large do not consider such fluctuations (in price) in the interest of local farmers, the industry, or the consumer.[m]

---

e National Coffee Association's efforts to identify ways to ensure an
iinable supply of coffee in the range of qualities demanded by
iile addressing social and ecological needs. We also support efforts
p of Excellence competitions that promote the host country's best

the National Coffee Association's position on the coffee crisis.
pared to support the International Coffee Organisation's scheme
it the NCA position.

Sara Lee is uneasy about price support. The market needs to equilibrate on supply and demand. We believe the best solution (is) ...to be found in the improvement of coffee quality at a local level.

Compensating coffee farmers for the burden of lower income by artificially paying guaranteed prices provides an incentive to over-production, while creating unwanted discriminating positions on the green coffee market. For this reason Sara Lee will not promote or initiate the marketing of coffee under the Fair Trade level. [m]

---

we have supported coffee growing countries on three levels:

utions from various P&G offices around the world, Brazil, Mexico
, to build schools.

- $1.5 million in funding to non-profit organisation, Technoserve,
:ale coffee growers.

G fund makes contributions to organizations like The Nature
id disaster relief efforts. [n]

Sara Lee's support includes "the execution of projects in coffee originating countries (Viet Nam, Uganda, Brazil) aimed at helping coffee farmers and their families to improve their living conditions by developing and implementing production-methods with minimal impact on the environment, while resulting in higher coffee quality and therefore in higher market prices." [o]

---

nificant portion of its total requirements directly from exporters
producing countries. The employees in our Green Coffee
end significant time in-country working with exporters; these
translate our local quality needs back through the local supply

While purchasing green coffee, Sara Lee will continue its Small Farmers Policy (since 1989), committing itself to a minimum of 10% of total coffee purchase being purchased directly through small planters and co-operations of small planters, preconditioned by the availability of required coffee qualities and related prices. [o]

---

e Social Responsibility July 2002
ut_pg/corporate/sustainability/faq
fam 11 June 2002

[l] Sustainable Coffee- document presented to Oxfam 11 June 2002
[m] Interview with Oxfam 10 June 2002

[n] Folgers Website, Procter & Gamble
[o] Sara Lee letter to Oxfam 19 June 2002

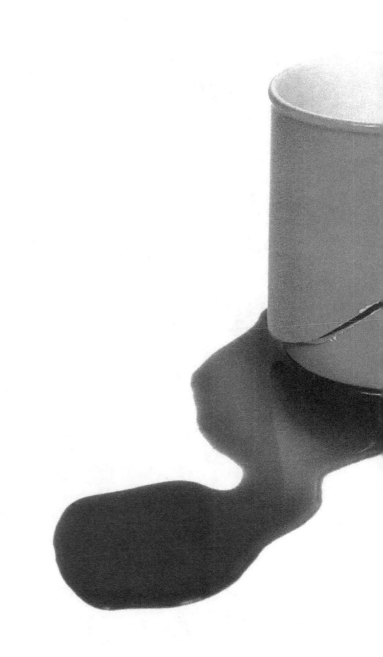

• Cost control

Another factor in roaster profitability is the way they manage their costs. Some of this has to do with technology. For instance, if a roaster is able to extract more soluble coffee from the coffee bean, this can help improve profits.

Another cost item for roasters is, obviously, the cost of the raw material: the green bean. But the importance of this cost varies greatly, depending on the company. For Nestlé, for example, which mainly makes and sells instant coffee, the cost of green beans is less important than it is for companies that sell roast and ground coffee. This is because Nestlé has to invest in expensive processing plants and manufacturing technology to create its products.

This has led Nestlé to argue, somewhat surprisingly, that low coffee bean prices are actually not in its business interest. The low price means that one part of its costs is reduced – and analysts Morgan Stanley estimate that *'...the benefits of lower coffee prices in 2001 must have been substantial.'*[48] However, the company claims that the overall impact can be negative. This is because its roast and ground competitors can cut their retail prices aggressively when coffee bean prices fall without worrying, as Nestlé has to, about covering large fixed costs such as soluble processing plants. *'The competitive position of soluble coffee such as Nescafé in relation to roast and ground coffee is less favourable in a low-price market,'*[49] claims the company. This is a major factor in Nestlé's recent statement concerning the desirability of higher and more stable coffee prices (see section 3).

Roast and ground companies may have more to gain from a fall in the bean price, but some of these benefits can be offset by bouts of competition as they wrestle for market share. What this means is that they may have to pass on cost savings to consumers in the form of lower prices. Sara Lee said in its nine-month results statement for 2002 that green coffee prices had led to lower retail prices. Combined with other issues (such as higher marketing expenditures), this had meant 'sales and operating income declines'. If tough times for Sara Lee yield a profit level for its beverages unit of nearly 17 per cent, imagine what the good times must be like.

• Mix and match: flexible blends

Roasters no longer need to hold large stocks of coffee, because contracts with international traders now guarantee them a ready supply of large volumes of different coffee types at relatively short notice. This allows them to mix and match their coffees and adjust their blends with increasing flexibility. Producer countries find themselves under even more pressure as roasters seek the lowest-cost combination of coffees to produce their standard blend. Stefano Ponte, in his analysis of the coffee markets in East Africa, writes: *'Ugandan robusta is threatened by the changing strategies of major roasters.... In general, international traders argue that roasters have achieved more flexibility in their blending processes and seem to be decreasingly committed to particular origins'.*[30]

• Futures markets: flexible financing

Roasters have extremely advanced ways to manage and minimise risks to their raw materials costs. Instead of paying the current market price, they construct contracts with traders that enable them to spread and hedge the risks of future price volatility. Complex mathematical modelling allows them to use futures markets through a simple click of a computer mouse, leading to agreements today on a price to be paid for coffee they will purchase in six to 18 months' time. Such financial tools allow them to optimise their purchasing strategies – a far cry from the severely limited market options facing producers.

New technology and techniques: driving down quality

New technologies and techniques in growing and processing are having worrying effects on both the quality of coffee and the environmental impacts of growing it. There has been a double decline in quality – first a move from arabica to lower-quality robusta, and second the quality of robusta itself has fallen.

These trends do not bode well for producers, for coffee drinkers or for the environmental sustainability of coffee production. Nor do they bode well for the roasters, particularly in as much as they affect their long-term supply base. They themselves acknowledge the problem. *'Our Millstone [P&G's premium brand] products are dependent on good quality beans. We are concerned about whether we will have coffee availability at all levels,'* Procter & Gamble has conceded.[51] And Nestlé agrees: *'The present low price situation has a tremendously negative impact on the quality of the coffee produced, making it more difficult for Nestlé to find the quality we need for our product,'* it has said.[52]

New roaster technology: squeezing the last drop out of the bean.

The roasters express concerns now about the decline in coffee quality. But they have developed technologies that mask the bitterness of the cheaper and lower-quality coffees, so enabling them to use more of them in their blends than they had previously been able to get away with. They were spurred on in this when the price of arabica spiked in 1997, giving them an incentive to find ways of getting more out of the robusta bean.

'Roasters have learned to increase the absorption of natural[53] and robusta coffees by such processes as steaming to remove the harshness of taste,' notes a report by USAID, the World Bank and the Inter-American Development Bank (IADB).[54]

Industry members acknowledge the importance of this shift. *'Increasing usage of low-quality/low-priced coffees (e.g. Viet Nam) mainly on the European continent and North America under competitive pressure is the only obvious fault by consuming countries,'* explains Paul Moeller of the Volcafe coffee trading company, in an analysis of the coffee crisis. One industry analyst estimates that, as an average percentage of coffee blends, robusta has increased from around 35 per cent to 40 per cent in the past five years (although it should be noted that Sara Lee states this not to be the case).

In some cases, the taste profile of entire countries has changed. Although Germany used to import mainly washed arabicas, it has seen a surge in imports of robusta and natural arabicas over the past decade.[55] Commenting on the growth of robusta imports, importer Bernhard Benecke said: *'The attraction was simply too big not to add a percentage more of robusta to your blend.'*[56]

It is not just the move to more robusta. There has also been a marked deterioration in the quality of that crop. Coffee buyers are interested in buying lower-grade coffee than before. In Uganda, for example, William Naggaga, board secretary of the Uganda Coffee Development Authority, says: *'Take coffee like black beans [the result of picking unripe cherries]. We never exported them until liberalisation. In the past, they were just thrown away. And then, it was the same buyers in Europe who said, "Well, we've got a use for black beans." We had to go to the Minister to allow us to include them as an export – because they were not an exportable grade in Uganda. We had to seek permission and a change of regulations to export black beans.'*[57]

Kraft's trading arm, Taloca, was the largest buyer of Vietnamese coffee in 2001, according to estimates from a US-based coffee importer. Last year, Taloca bought nearly 1.2m bags of Vietnamese coffee, just ahead of Neumann, another big trading company.

Kraft acknowledges the importance of quality: *'In the current situation of worldwide high coffee production and stagnating consumption, quality will be an ever more important issue in a trade-driven market.'*[58] The company is also remarkably candid about the quality problems it found in Viet Nam. In particular, it is concerned about the fact that '...*severe quality and environmental problems can be stated within all stages of the coffee production process [in Viet Nam]...*'.

These problems include strip-picking: '*As strip-picking is common practice with robusta, the percentage of green immature cherries is high, which makes proper drying more difficult and time-consuming,*' it notes. The warm and humid climate in Viet Nam aggravates the situation. These conditions, according to Kraft, lead to 'cup quality deterioration'. Further problems in previous years have included 'yellow-leaf disease', which has been reported in some parts of the country and results partly from over-fertilisation. Kraft describes how in Viet Nam incomplete drying techniques on the farm make it necessary to re-dry the coffee before export. '*[The re-drying] is done by wood, coal, or sometimes even rubber tyres, which possibly affects the coffee as the unpleasant rubber smell in some cases is absorbed.*'

Although Kraft has developed a quality improvement scheme in Viet Nam, this is not targeting the robusta-producing regions (e.g. Dak Lak) as this '*would require huge financial support at low expectation of success due to largeness of production areas, extent of problems and already fixed infrastructure*'. Instead Kraft and its partners are focusing on improved arabica.[59]

Too much robusta, too little arabica

Viet Nam's entry into the big league of coffee producers has certainly helped to skew world coffee production towards robusta, since that is what the country overwhelmingly grows. But it is not alone. Brazil, still mainly an arabica producer, has more than doubled its robusta output over the past ten years to nearly 11m bags.[60]

The paradox is that while the coffee market is awash with robusta, supplies of higher-quality arabica are actually being squeezed: there is too much cheap coffee depressing prices in the mainstream market and too little quality coffee at the specialty end. As the graph below shows, supplies of arabica have actually fallen, as a proportion of overall supplies (figure 10).[61]

Figure 10: Robusta rises arabica falls
World production shares, %

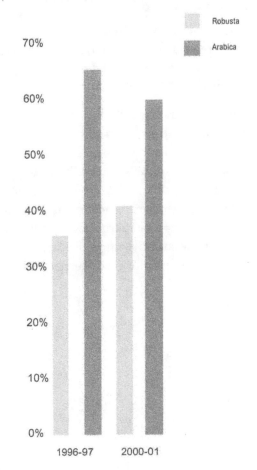

This increase in intensive robusta production has hit poor, smallholder coffee farmers hardest. Robusta comes in different varieties (a Vietnamese robusta is different from an Indian robusta, for example) but those differences are not highly prized by consumers or the big buyers of coffee. It is a different situation with arabica, as consumers will pay more to drink a pure arabica coffee from Ethiopia, Colombia or Costa Rica.

As a result, producers of robusta find they are increasingly competing on price – so in sub-Saharan Africa, for instance, where productivity levels are low compared with Viet Nam or Brazil, farmers are not covering even their most basic costs. Nor can they simply shift into growing the generally more profitable arabica: it is a delicate crop that requires high altitudes and many farmers may also lack the skills and inputs needed to grow it.

Intensive farming techniques reduce quality and degrade the land

Greater competition among suppliers has spurred the use of more intensive coffee-farming techniques, threatening to reduce quality and degrade the environment.

Coffee estates have traditionally harvested selectively, with strict quality controls to ensure that only ripe cherries are picked. But as prices have dropped, so have these standards: strip-picking and late harvesting have become increasingly common. Strip-picking cherries from trees in whole clusters, instead of plucking them individually, mixes ripe and unripe together; harvesting late – to save on the cost of multiple pickings – mixes black or decaying beans with good cherries, leading to mould formation.

Intensive techniques are threatening the longer-term sustainability of coffee production. In many countries, coffee has traditionally been planted amongst shade trees, interspersed with other food or cash crops. This process not only conserves soil and forest, but protects the micro-climate. In Central America, it also creates an important habitat for migratory birds. Intensification has led to the removal of shade to promote higher yields, with full-sun coffee grown in mono-crop stands, and the planting of fast-developing dwarf hybrid varieties that give better yields in response to greater use of agrochemicals. In Brazil, for example, government constraints on tree density and planting techniques have been lifted.[62] Tree-planting has become far denser, increasing from the traditional 900-1,200 coffee trees per hectare to 5,000-8,000. Producers in a number of countries now widely use these techniques to produce higher-volume, lower-cost coffee.[63]

The scientific body, CABI Commodities, confirms the changes taking place: *'Fast-developing dwarf hybrid varieties, whose yields respond vigorously to fertiliser applications; rust-resistant varieties that lower input costs; shade removal that stimulates yield increases; and mechanisation that has allowed coffee production in Brazil to move away from frost-prone populated areas to more northerly, frost-free, low-populated regions are all recent changes. Intensive production methods were promoted by donors, especially in Central America, part of a worldwide trend towards more intensive farming.'*[64]

Such intensive techniques have produced unprecedented yields, but many observers question whether they are sustainable and argue that they should not be taken as a productivity benchmark for others to follow.

No alternatives: declining commodities and the failures of rural development

Poor coffee farmers are struggling. The costs of switching out of coffee are substantial and farmers lack feasible alternatives to turn to – partly because of the failure of international aid donors and national governments to promote rural development and diversification, and partly due to the protectionist policies of the EU and US, which have effectively prevented developing-country farmers from benefiting from other commodities. This means that too many are now depending on too few options. Additionally, like all farmers, coffee producers face longstanding problems of rural underdevelopment: poor transport infrastructure, lack of credit, very restricted direct access to markets and therefore limited information about the best possible prices.

Lack of alternatives to coffee as a cash crop

Despite calls for several decades for diversification away from commodity dependence, it has not happened in many countries: sub-Saharan Africa, for instance, is now more dependent on commodities than it was 20 years ago.[65] This is a stunning policy failure at every level.

It may seem economically irrational for farmers to continue to sell coffee at a price that does not allow them to cover their basic needs, but in fact the decision is entirely rational. First, the costs of replacing their coffee trees with an alternative crop are high. Even if their land is suitable for, say cocoa, they may lack the skills or training to grow it, and most farming families have no savings to live off while waiting for the new crops to bear fruit.

Second, there is a severe lack of compelling alternatives. Coffee farmers know better than most how dangerous it is to rely wholly on this fickle crop for their income and so most smallholders intercrop their coffee with subsistence and other cash crops, or raise chicken and cattle. Domestic markets for their produce tend to be too small and too low-priced to replace the income that coffee used to generate: the returns on many alternative crops are as bad as coffee, or worse. Abarya Abadura, a coffee farmer from Jimma in Ethiopia says: *'Three years ago I received $105 a year from my corn. Last year, I received $35.'* The price paid for corn – a key staple – is estimated to have fallen over 60 per cent in the last five years. Abarya explains the connection: *'When the coffee price falls, people don't have enough money to buy corn.'*[66]

Depending on declining commodities

Coffee is not alone in its crisis: many commodities, such as sugar, rice and cotton, face long-term price declines as increased productivity and greater competition increase their supply beyond demand (figure 11). Like coffee, many of these other commodities are experiencing the boom and bust of volatile prices.

This long-term decline is not only closing down alternatives for farmers, it is also devastating national economies. The greater a country's reliance on primary commodities, the more devastating the impact of falling prices on government budgets. Commodity dependency has worsened in sub-Saharan Africa, with 17 countries depending on non-oil commodity exports for 75 per cent or more of their export earnings.[67] Many of these countries still face heavy debt burdens and their capacity to repay has been severely undermined.

The World Bank and the IMF have exacerbated this problem with the 'one size fits all' approach that they have pushed onto all low-income countries, using structural adjustment lending. This approach has focused on the need to generate export-led growth and to facilitate foreign investment through liberalising trade barriers, devaluing exchange rates, and privatising state enterprises – essentially moving to a free market situation, where each country supposedly develops its own 'comparative advantage'. However, little attention is paid to the direct impact of this approach on poor people.

Historically, the lowest-income countries have depended on producing primary commodities, and in many cases the focus on liberalisation and comparative advantage has increased that dependence. At the same time, the removal of tariffs or support to domestic industry in the interests of a fully free market has made it increasingly difficult for countries to diversify 'upstream' or into more value-added industrial enterprises. Attempts to try and protect new industries have met strong opposition from the World Bank and the IMF: Ugandan programmes, for example, to promote strategic export areas such as fish processing and protect this infant industry, have *'been met with derision by World Bank and IMF officials'.*[68]

Figure 11: Real non-oil commodity prices

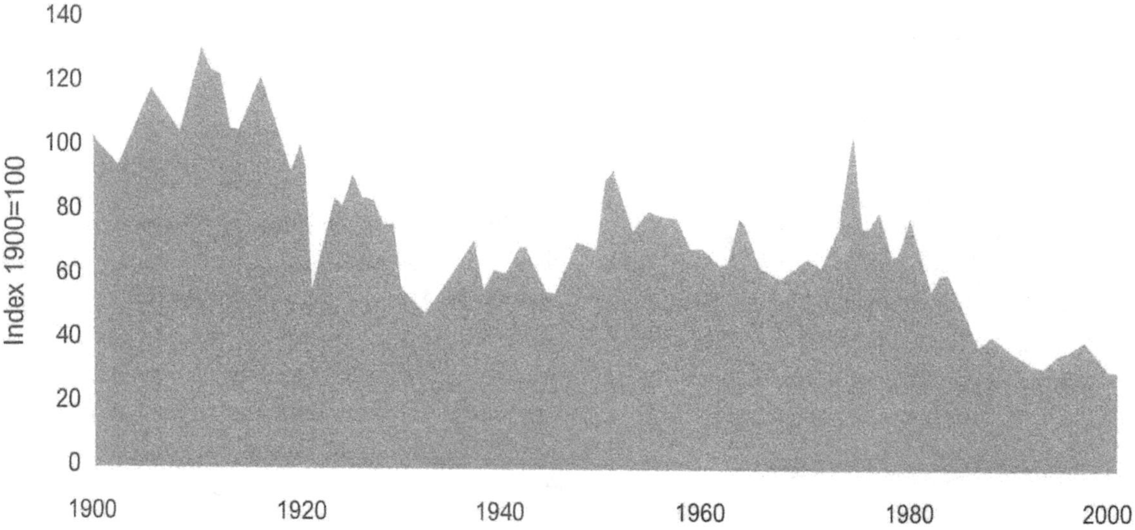

Source: World Bank

Too little value captured

Far too little processing and packaging of coffee takes place in producer countries, which means that very little of the potential value of the coffee bean is captured. In 2000/01, a staggering 94 per cent of all coffee exported from developing countries crossed the border in its green bean state: most of the remaining six per cent that had been processed came from Brazil, India, and Colombia.[69]

The low value added in coffee is a problem that dogs many commodities. A recent consultation on commodities at the FAO concluded, among other things, that: *'The producers' share of prices is unusually low and they appear to be lowest in commodities that have highly concentrated food-processing sectors. Thus it appears that the market structure is an important area which needs investigation. The benefits of better market information were discussed as a way to improve the bargaining position of commodity exporters.'*[70]

Increased processing of coffee in the country of origin is essential to raise returns – but for most countries the barriers are high. Building a processing plant for soluble coffee comes with a price tag of $20m-plus, though roasting and grinding is cheaper. Even if processing in developing countries were affordable, the absence of other locally produced inputs, such as quality packaging, raises other obstacles. One alternative is to encourage transnationals to invest in producing countries but most, Nestlé apart (Sara Lee also has an important presence in Brazil, a big coffee consumer), choose not to: their highly efficient plants in the US and Europe represent a sunk cost and are also closer to the end consumer, an important consideration for some types of coffee.

Barriers are high in distribution too. Much coffee is sold as a blend from many origins. Trade links between producer countries are not generally strong, and this hampers their ability to develop their own regional blends. Existing brands from developing countries generally lack the recognition and profile of competing lines, and breaking through the well-established relationships between major roasters and retailers is a hard battle. It is not impossible, however: Ismael Andrade, an exporter of a popular Brazilian coffee, Sabor de Minas, has successfully marketed coffee to some of the world's biggest retail chains, including Wal-Mart and Carrefour.[71]

Unlike the case of many agricultural products, import tariffs into rich-country markets are not the main barrier for most coffee producers. There are no import tariffs on processed coffee, whether roasted or soluble, coming into the US, for example. Processed coffee can enter the EU tax-free from all African, Caribbean and Pacific countries, as well as many countries in Latin America (including Colombia, El Salvador, Guatemala, Honduras, and Nicaragua). But other poor countries, such as India, Viet Nam, and East Timor, pay 3.1 per cent import duty on soluble and 2.6 per cent on roast and ground coffee, while Brazil and Thailand pay tariffs of up to nine per cent on soluble.[72]

International traders are increasingly active in producer countries. Roaster companies rely on these traders to supply very large volumes of coffee from diverse origins at short notice. This has changed the way traders work, according to Stefano Ponte: *'The need to guarantee the constant supply of a variety of origins and coffee types has prompted international traders to get even more involved in producing countries than they would have done simply as a result of market liberalisation.'*[73]

With fewer restrictions on foreign investment, international traders have either established local subsidiaries or now deal directly with producers – in rare cases they own the coffee farms themselves. Some of these traders have very close links with the major roasters. This shift is confirmed by Lorenzo Castillo, of Peru's Junta Nacional de Café, who says: *'The transnational companies want to reduce costs. To do so they are seeking to reduce intermediaries between themselves and the producer. The most vulnerable to substitution are the exporters.... The hook, for the producer, is the provision of credit.'*[74]

Local millers, middlemen and even larger domestic trading companies are struggling to stay afloat as they do not have the financial resources of the international trading houses to hold out through the slump. In Uganda, for example, the number of exporters has shrunk from 150 to 20 over the past decade, according to one European trader, and many of those who have lost out have been local entrepreneurs.

This has left a gap that the better capitalised and stronger international traders have stepped into. In Tanzania, for instance, Stefano Ponte notes that transnationals now *'control more than half of the export market through direct subsidiaries, and another substantial proportion through finance agreements with local companies'.*[75] The concern is that the crisis is undermining an important local entrepreneurial base while the profits generated for the international trading companies flow back to industrialised countries.

Failure to deliver on rural development

The deregulation of international coffee markets has been mirrored by the liberalisation of domestic markets in many producer countries, often pushed by IMF and World Bank policies. Parastatal coffee organisations, which in many cases acted as monopoly buyers of coffee, have been gradually dismantled or privatised. Taxes and other levies on coffee have been lowered and state control over coffee production reduced. Many restrictions on foreign investment and ownership have been lifted, particularly in trading and export sectors.

For farmers there have been some benefits to deregulation: in many countries they are capturing a larger proportion of the export price of their coffee. Professor Christopher Gilbert explains: *'Liberalisation raises the farmers' share of the FOB [export] price by reducing costs in the marketing chain, and because it has often been associated with a reduction in taxation and other levies and so affords less opportunity for rent extraction.'*[76] Yet this benefit has paled into insignificance in the face of the overall fall in the price of coffee.

At the same time, farmers have faced many harmful consequences. Where government services have pulled out, markets have largely failed to step in: no surprise for a crisis commodity. At a time when farmers are more exposed to the vagaries of the market than ever before, their vulnerability has been compounded by cutbacks in support services and a paucity of alternative sources of help, resulting in a lower quality of the coffee they can grow and even less power in the market.

Inadequate regulation

Some experts believe that the loosening of controls over coffee production has contributed to the decline in quality, especially of the arabicas, which require more care and inputs.

According to Professor Christopher Gilbert: *'Market organisation issues are very important in arabica production, much more than in robusta. Full liberalisation does appear to adversely affect quality [for arabica]. The best arabica is produced in countries where some degree of regulation is permitted [Colombia, Costa Rica, Kenya]. ... My personal view is that arabica farmers can do best in a mixed system with strong co-operatives [Kenya] or state bodies [Colombia]. Independent regulation is crucial.'*[77]

Farmers' and workers' organisation under attack

Many of the supposed benefits of deregulation depend on supportive institutions and organisations that do not exist. Not only have support services been cut back; the civil-society organisations that might press for the building of small farmers' capacities to make new market linkages, have also been weakened.

Research from recent experience in Ethiopia shows how independent farmers' co-operatives, if well run, can play a vital role in setting a floor price for coffee. Co-operatives can also help bypass middlemen and gain access to high-value export markets. The result can be higher returns to individual farmers, plus the funding of important community services. Any public-policy decision to support such structures should address the fact that restrictions on women's participation in co-operatives may leave them less able to take advantage of the opportunities to capture value that co-operative membership can offer.

Scarce information

Many farmers suffer from a lack of information – from current prices to new harvesting techniques – so reducing the quality and price of their produce. The Uganda Coffee Development Authority (UCDA) used to broadcast coffee prices on eight radio stations but the programme was cut back, in part due to low coffee prices. There are plans to resume it but farmers have meanwhile lost valuable information. The Honduras Coffee Institute reports that farmers are systematically missing out on any upward jump in the coffee price.[78] In Ethiopia, the same: exporters knew in April 2002 that the price had picked up,[79] but farmers did not and missed out on their share of improved prices.

Too little training and support

Technical know-how is crucial for increasing yields and adding value. Studies suggest that smallholder coffee yields in some producing countries in Africa are very low: under 500kg per hectare. Compare that with the average 1500-2000 kg/ha in Viet Nam. The difference is not only that there are lower inputs in Africa, but also less know-how on pruning cycles, weeding and mulching. In some countries, cutbacks in extension services have meant less timely spraying against pests and have led to greater problems with diseases. Lack of technical know-how also reduces quality if farmers do not know how to produce a better-quality cherry or increase value through basic processing.

Bad loans, no new credit

The price slump has left many farmers unable to pay off their loans. A survey of Vietnamese coffee farmers indicates that more than 60 per cent have large outstanding loans.[80] The need to pay off debts often means that farmers can't wait for an upturn and have to take the going price offered by the traders. Carmela Rodriguez, a 56-year-old farmer from Sauce, Peru, says: *'By word of mouth, we hear that sometimes prices are better in Tarapoto or in Moyobamba or in Jaen. But for us, it is difficult to take [our coffee] there. And we can't warehouse it there because of all our debts. We can't afford to.'*[81]

Rising bad debts mean shrinking new credit – indeed rural credit has dried up in many countries. When co-operatives are stuck for credit, farmers have to turn to local traders. According to Mohammed Indris, a coffee farmer in Ethiopia: *'The co-operative purchases keep the price up. Last year, the co-operative was not able to buy red cherry as it had financial difficulties. When the private traders realised this, they dropped their prices from US$0.11 cents/kg to $0.06/kg.'*[82]

The lack of credit leaves farmers particularly exposed in the harsh months before harvest. Some can get food on credit in exchange for their coming crop; others use their land as collateral – though not all farmers have title deeds to their property. Others still are reduced to selling off their assets. Women are particularly disadvantaged as land ownership structures often prevent them from holding titles to land. This makes it more difficult for them to obtain credit.

Weak rural infrastructure

The longstanding lack of investment in rural transport in many countries has resulted in very high costs, especially for smallholder farmers who do not have enough bags of coffee to justify the cost of a pick-up to take their unprocessed cherries to the local mill. Even where pick-ups are used, the costs per kilometre are far higher than on bigger roads: Oxfam research in Uganda found that the cost of transporting a bag of coffee just 15km to the local milling station was not much cheaper proportionally than transporting the same bag 100km from the milling station to Kampala.

The absence of good roads presents very real hardship for farmers. This is what one has to say: *'I am Avelios Asuego. I am a small farmer of organic coffee from Guatemala. I would like to tell you a bit of my personal story. We have to go for four hours by foot to get to the paved road from my community, which gives you a sense of how isolated we are from the modern world. From there, we have to go another three hours by car, which is a rough ride because the conditions of our roads are very poor. Three hours takes us to where we park and leave our coffee to be marketed.'[83]*

Inadequate access to basic facilities such as drying tables and processing mills harms the quality of the farmer's produce. Most smallholders sun-dry their coffee – but without access to basic solar-drying tables, or the know-how to build them, they end up spreading the beans directly on the ground. Arabica coffee cherries should be processed as soon as possible after picking. However, when small-scale processing mills are not locally available, smallholders have to harvest a sufficient volume before transporting them – and that delay can cause the cherries to become mouldy.

Declining aid and double standards: farmers betrayed by the donors

Donor countries have contributed directly to this crisis, first by deeply neglecting investment in rural development, second by exacerbating the situation with double standards that have encouraged developing countries to liberalise, while still using heavy protectionism to block them out of rich-country markets, squeezing their options into a narrow range of commodities. The result is a glaring betrayal of agricultural opportunities in developing countries.

Support for rural development – vital for millions of farmers in the world's poorest countries – has been declining, as shown in figure 12. The OECD points out the failing commitment of its own member countries: *'Aid to agriculture, already stagnating in the early 1980s, declined from 1985 at an annual average rate of seven per*

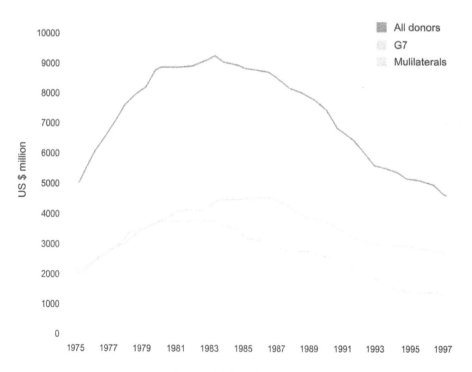

Figure 12: Declining aid to agriculture: 1973-2000

Five-year moving average, constant 1999 prices

All donors
G7
Mulilaterals

US $ million

Source: CRS and DAC statistics

cent. As a result, aid to agriculture fell from a 17 per cent share in the early 1980s to eight per cent at the end of the 1990s. The decline is partly explained by cuts in ODA in general but donors' sectoral policies have also changed [from agriculture and other productive sectors towards the social sectors]. It is plausible that the exclusion of agriculture from the poverty reduction agenda of the 1990s explains some of the decline.'[84]

Given the dependence of so many poor people on agriculture for their livelihoods, this decline is appalling. *'By OECD estimates, Overseas Development Assistance to agriculture now represents eight per cent of total ODA: eight per cent to support three-quarters of the poor,'* says Lennart Bage, President of the UN's International Fund for Agricultural Development.[85]

Rich countries have displayed a really deft touch for double standards on trade recently. The most egregious example has been the US's new farm bill. In 2000, rich countries subsidised their farmers to the extent of $245bn.[86] Current subsidy patterns, with their emphasis on expanding production, have devastating effects on poor farmers in developing countries. This is because these subsidies distort the market and enable rich-country farmers to sell their produce at very low prices on world markets. Poor farmers cannot compete on such unfair terms.

Rich countries also impose tariff barriers on goods that many developing countries depend upon for export revenues: agricultural and labour-intensive manufactured products. Import tariffs cost developing countries around $43bn a year.[87]

The unfair subsidies and import tariffs of rich countries have an impact on coffee farmers: they limit the range of options that they can move into and are therefore part of the wider problem of commodities. A Wall Street Journal article on Nicaragua makes the point: *'Other [coffee] farmers talk of switching crops. They are discouraged, however, by the experience of farmers who have grown peanuts and sesame. Those growers now find themselves on the verge of bankruptcy after trying to compete against US farmers receiving generous subsidies from Washington.'*[88]

Countries in sub-Saharan Africa are most acutely hit. Their governments have put forward a plan of action with the New Partnership for Africa's Development (NEPAD). The response from rich-country governments has been disappointing.

Niche markets – an escape route?
Not for all…

3

Maria, Janet, Eduarda and Felicia taking a coffee break at Chiclayo coffee processing factory in Piura, Peru. The factory supplies coffee beans to Cafédirect for the Fair Trade market.

3. Niche markets – an escape route? Not for all...

In contrast with the mainstream price slump, niche, or 'specialty', coffees – new types of coffee drink sold at a premium – have been a runaway success. Sellers distinguish these coffees by highlighting their country of origin, by emphasising their particular characteristics, or by showing a commitment to organic, shade-grown or Fair Trade practices. The farmers who can sell into these markets often get a much better price for their crop.

The pioneers of these popular alternatives have not been the traditional roasters but the coffee bars that have made latte, cappuccino, and espresso familiar to Western customers. One of the biggest chains, Starbucks, has declared its intention to both source all its coffee from farmers who meet new social and environmental guidelines and to buy 74 per cent of its green coffee at fixed, long-term prices, thus guaranteeing stability and predictability for coffee farmers in 2002. What is interesting about these measures is that the business case that argues that these measures are needed to guarantee coffee quality appears to have been put to, and accepted by, investors. Consumers will be interested to see whether small farmers reap any benefit from this scheme.

Here and there, co-operatives in producing countries are teaming up with specialty coffee traders and outlets in consumer countries to change the way coffee is bought and sold. In Nicaragua, for instance, two small farms recently sold their special arabica via an internet auction for $11.75/lb, about 23 times the New York price.[89] A key part of developing these special coffees and disseminating information about them is to hold competitions that reward the best quality.

Better prices and a premium on quality make niche markets particularly attractive for farmers and countries seeking to escape that low-price, low-quality trap.

Success stories are often held up as a beacon of hope for the rest looking for a way out. Crucially, however, governments and industry have to appreciate the danger of encouraging everyone to run for the same exit. A niche market will lose its special status and its ability to pay high prices if it is swamped and if its consumer market does not grow with it.

Fair Trade: a glimmer of hope

'In coffee the Fair Trade movement has clearly shown that producers can be paid double today's disastrously low prices without affecting the consumer's willingness to buy a good-quality product.' – Pablo Dubois, Head of Operations, International Coffee Organisation

In the current climate, Fair Trade has become a lifeline for many producers. Fair Trade has given rise to many commercial businesses which operate at a profit but which retain the explicit development objectives of improving the lives of the farmers from whom they buy. At the heart of Fair Trade is a central principle: a commitment to pay farmers a fair price – one that covers costs and is stable. Arabica farmers, for example, are currently paid a minimum of $1.26/lb,[90] which is well over double the market price.

The first fairly traded coffee was imported into the Netherlands in 1973 from Guatemalan small-farmer co-operatives. Thirty years later, nearly 200 coffee co-operatives representing 675,000 farmers, more than 70 traders and around 350 coffee companies work to the standards of Fairtrade Labelling Organisations International (FLO), to bring products to market in a way that ensures the farmers receive a decent return.

With a strong emphasis on co-operative management and organisational structures, Fair Trade requires people in the coffee supply chain to work to transparent terms of trade and to guarantee decent production conditions, at the same time as addressing some of the key obstacles that prevent poor farmers from accessing markets. These include measures such as partial pre-financing of orders to avoid small producer organisations falling into debt; payment of a premium for use by mutual agreement between producers; contractual commitments that allow farmers to make provision for long-term production planning; and the guarantee of social and environmental conditions that reflect International Labour Organisation conventions on working conditions.

The FLO standard for coffee is a voluntary scheme, paid for by licence fees levied on the brand owners. The guarantee of decent terms and conditions for farmers is monitored by FLO in co-operation with national bodies, while organisations such as Max Havelaar (the Netherlands, Belgium, France, Switzerland, Denmark), TransFair USA (North America), and the Fairtrade Foundation (UK) manage and promote the different certification marks in their respective consumer markets.

The most important impact of Fair Trade has been on the lives of farmers who have been able to sell their coffee at prices that meet their basic needs. At the Oromiya Coffee Farmers Co-operative Union in Ethiopia, for example, farmers can get 70 per cent of the export price for coffee that sells as Fair Trade, while those in the Jimma zone of Ethiopia's Kafa province, selling in the open market, get only 30 per cent.

Felipe Huaman of the Bagua Grande Co-operative in Peru, which sells to the Fair Trade market, explains: *'Ever since our alliance with Twin and Cafédirect our prices have started improving and this has improved living conditions for the coffee growers' families. This is our biggest reward and what we most appreciate.'* The improved price is certainly significant, but one study indicates that the indirect benefits in terms of farmer organisation may be even more important.[91]

Secondly, Fair Trade has beneficial impacts on the environment. The focus on small producers and the emphasis on sustainable production techniques means that the majority of Fair Trade coffee is shade-grown, with all the biodiversity advantages this offers over sun-grown coffee. The coffee pulp produced by the first stage of processing continues to be used as mulch on the crop, thus avoiding decreasing oxygen levels and the pollution of rivers.

Thirdly, Fair Trade provides the threat of a good example to the big coffee firms. By indirectly highlighting the fact that farmers supplying the mainstream market are paid prices that do not even cover production costs, the very existence of the Fair Trade movement has posed a serious reputation risk to companies whose products are very susceptible to consumer sensibilities.

As Kraft recognises, *'Since the beginning of the 1990s an increasing number of trade organisation[s] became active, offering coffee brands under various 'fair trade' or 'ecologically friendly' labels, thus competing [with] the conventional coffee business with ethically based arguments. Since the demand for 'fair traded' ... products so far is only moderate ... this has created only minor business but major image problems for the traditional coffee industry as a whole.'*[92]

Initially the mainstream coffee companies objected strongly to the term 'Fair Trade', due to its implication that other goods were traded unfairly: Nestlé went so far as to produce a leaflet countering the Fair Trade claims. This was followed by a switch in attitude to 'if you can't beat them, join them' and moves by some companies to buy a small percentage of their coffee from Fair Trade producers, or at least to pay a premium over the market rate.

Companies now argue that their Fair Trade lines remain small because demand for them is limited – but demand can be developed and expanded, as these owners of major brands know so well. When given the choice, consumers are increasingly opting for the ethical choice: worldwide, Fair Trade coffee sales grew by 12 per cent in 2001[93] compared with overall growth in coffee consumption of just 1.5 per cent.

Fair Trade roast and ground coffee now accounts for

over seven per cent of the UK roast and ground market and about two per cent of the total coffee market. Cafédirect, a leading Fairtrade brand in which Oxfam has an equity stake, now ranks in sixth position in the UK coffee market – streets ahead of Italian brand Lavazza.[94] In the last three years, over 140 companies have begun to sell Fair Trade-certified products in the US through an estimated 10,000 retail outlets nationwide: market growth was 36 per cent in 2001 alone.

The main criticism of Fair Trade comes from those economists who believe that the high prices it offers lead farmers who would be better off seeking alternatives to stay in coffee production, exacerbating long-term oversupply. Oxfam believes that, whether or not Fair Trade can be applied in the mainstream, the lack of alternatives and the absence of government safety nets for poor producers make this sort of support to farmers an entirely justifiable and appropriate attempt to cope with the human cost of the rigours of the free market.

Despite its success, it will be impossible for Fair Trade alone to provide a solution to the crisis because of the persisting imbalance between supply and demand. This does not mean that mainstream firms cannot make a more substantive commitment to buying fairly traded coffee: they can and should. What it does mean, however, is that broader initiatives to address the current imbalances in the mainstream market are also needed.

Specialty brands capturing high value

Some producer countries have benefited from the specialty market by branding the quality coffee from their country or its regions and successfully developing a name and niche market. Jamaica has cultivated its Blue Mountain brand of coffee and India its Monsooned Malabar, both of which are highly prized. Colombia is held up as another big success story in this regard: its large investment in marketing, coupled with the provision of extension services to farmers, has produced

quality coffee sold at a premium under the Juan Valdez and Café de Colombia brand names. But even this success has hit hard times. As coffee revenues have dwindled, the coffee authorities in Colombia have had to cut back on the marketing of Juan Valdez.

Running for the same exit?

Initiatives that help producers target the premium end of the market make sense, since that is the one part of the market in rich countries that is growing. However, it is vital that companies and governments – both of consumer and producer countries – acknowledge that this can only be one part of an overall solution.

Not all poor producers can move into the premium market of specialty arabica coffees. If too many producers try to move into this segment of the market, it would cease to be a niche capable of commanding high prices. Simply supporting producers in the specialty market cannot be a solution to the systemic problems affecting millions of farmers. The problem of everyone running for the same exit – known in economics as 'the fallacy of composition' – has been a hallmark of commodity production for decades, and one that has not been sufficiently tackled by international institutions.

The World Bank and the IMF have contributed to the coffee crisis here too, by their failure to advise coffee-producing countries adequately on the impact of increased production on world prices. The World Bank has a unit dedicated to tracking and predicting world commodity prices[95] but its predictions are consistently over-optimistic, giving producer countries misleading signals about future market improvements. The World Bank and the IMF have recently produced a paper which estimates that the loss of export earnings due to the decline in commodity prices could amount to 1.5-2 per cent of GDP for the 24 Heavily Indebted Poor Countries during 2000 and 2001.[96] They have also called for additional funding from donors to enable top-up payments for countries suffering from shocks such as collapsing commodity prices. Donor governments must come up with the money now.

In addition, it is central to the roles of the international financial institutions to advise borrower governments on the risks and drawbacks of increasing production and to suggest alternative strategies. They have, however, consistently failed to do this. In Burundi, for example, where coffee accounts for 80 per cent of export earnings, the World Bank recently produced a report which failed to identify the risk of the country's enormous reliance on coffee, despite a whole section discussing other potential risks;[97] another of its reports identifies coffee as 'a source of growth'.[98]

Similarly, in Ethiopia, the Joint Staff Assessment of the Interim Poverty Reduction Strategy Paper (PRSP), prepared by the IMF and World Bank, does not raise the issue of over-reliance on coffee, despite a consideration of this clearly being absent from the government's plans for 'Agriculture Development-Led Industrialisation'.[99]

No grounds for inertia

The major roasters have failed seriously to tackle the problem of the low-price, low-quality rut in which the coffee market is stuck – surely exposing them to a core business risk. Some have made *ad hoc* and limited moves on quality or environment issues, but these fall far short of the scale of the initiative needed to tackle this crisis. The contrast with the political energy expended by rich companies and governments seeking movement on the 'new issues' of investment and competition rules at the next round of World Trade Organisation talks is striking.

Nestlé alone has spoken out about the need for a co-ordinated and international approach to manage supply in coffee. 'Nestlé is against low prices as they are not only bad for farmers, but also bad for Nestlé's business ... Nestlé therefore supports initiatives aimed at better managing supply, reducing volatility, and maintaining coffee prices within price bands that provide a satisfactory livelihood for producers and allow consumption to grow. This includes arrangements similar to the International Coffee Agreement.'[100]

All the companies have been slow to recognise that they have any responsibilities for addressing the plight of farmers, and some still deny this to be the case. A toe was dangled over the water in the form of the National Coffee Association of USA's global summit in February 2002, entitled *In Search of Global Solutions*, which identified eight options for the industry to consider when addressing the problem. The options included farmer education on crop diversification, roaster use of long-term, independently arrived at contracts, and increased accessibility, convenience, and quality choices for coffee consumers. A palpable lack of urgency surrounded the event: the board meeting to discuss prioritising three of those eight options took place three months later.

While it is true that there are no easy solutions, complexity is no excuse for inertia. The World Bank warns, *'If current trends continue as predicted by many, a coffee crisis could evolve into a broad social and environmental crisis.'*[101] To avoid this, a concerted international effort is needed, which brings together all the major players in the coffee trade, plus those organisations able to bring a development dimension to the table. Different actors will be able to assume different, complementary, roles. Most important, it is time for global trade leaders and the big coffee roasters to get involved.

Rupert Elvin

4

Getting out of crisis: a strategy for action

Oxfam's vision of a coffee market that works for the poor calls for action, by many players, on five fronts:

- restore the balance of supply and demand
- restore quality and raise productivity
- raise prices, revive livelihoods
- retain and build value-adding capacity
- establish real alternatives for rural development.

Immediate action is needed to break out of the slump but new, longer-term policies and practices are also needed to support farmers through the transition as the market comes back into balance.

Governments and multilateral agencies need to speak out, now, on the coffee crisis. They need to galvanise political support for the argument that the price fall in coffee and other commodities is a vital trade issue – even if the largely unregulated coffee market is not primarily a WTO issue – and call on rich countries to address this argument with the same vigour they approach investment or services. These same trade officials need to bring pressure to bear on the coffee giants to demonstrate corporate social responsibility and enlightened self-interest by committing themselves to a role in resolving the crisis.

Restore the balance of supply and demand

As an immediate priority, governments and companies need to commit to financing the destruction of 5m bags of the lowest-quality coffee currently held in importing country stocks. This would cost roughly $100m. This action would send an immediate signal to the market and, according to economic analysis conducted for the International Coffee Organisation, could lead to a price rise of 20 per cent on 2000/01 average prices –

providing between $700m and $800m in additional export income for coffee-producing countries.[102]

There is real potential for the roasters to do more in terms of what even they accept as their role: expanding and developing the coffee market. Their performance in this respect has been dismal: they have presided over big losses of beverage market share in rich countries such as the US. They could give far more attention to developing new consumer demand in emerging markets, rather than fighting over their share of traditional US and European customers.

In the longer term, much more collaboration is needed between different players to find market-based mechanisms that will prevent supply and demand from becoming so out of balance. This will require international leadership to bring all the parties together. The resulting agreement must include market intervention to manage supply.

Restore quality and raise productivity

Restoring quality is central to restoring value to the coffee bean. The most significant proposal addressing the crisis at the international level is the ICO Coffee Quality Improvement Scheme, to be implemented towards the end of 2002, which aims to stop the export of coffee that falls below a certain quality.

If this scheme were implemented in full it could remove between three and five per cent of all coffee produced from the international market and end the current destructive drive of low-quality incentives. The scheme needs financial backing, especially to evaluate its impact on poor farmers and poor countries, and it will need to ensure that support is given to poor producers of the lowest-quality coffee – particularly farmers with limited technologies and countries with limited internal markets.

Small farmers often have the potential to produce very good-quality coffee because they can be more careful about picking ripe cherries than can the operators of larger, mechanised plantations. But there are many other determinants of quality with which smaller farmers need help, as well as structures to ensure that they get rewarded for the quality they produce. Examples include help with good processing practices, help with technical and marketing skills, and improved negotiating clout through producer organisations.

Countries with very limited internal markets for coffee will need support because they will not be able to export their lowest-quality coffee under the ICO scheme, and neither will this surplus coffee be easily absorbed by domestic buyers.

The ICO quality scheme is a critically important initiative on the part of the producer countries, but it has not been given the backing it needs from roasters and consumer country governments. Their support – through their purchasing and monitoring of imports – will be essential to make the scheme successful in the commercial mainstream.

Raising the productivity of farmers at the bottom of the pile – for example, robusta farmers in a number of sub-Saharan countries – may be necessary. Any government support in this direction, however, should be careful not to compound the problem of oversupply. Increases in productivity that use less land to produce the same amount of coffee as before can have the net result of freeing up land or cash for alternative uses, giving farmers more options without increasing oversupply.

Examples of what can be done include a programme undertaken by the Ugandan Coffee Development Authority to provide free seedlings of a more productive coffee hybrid – an initiative that is credited with having helped make Ugandan farmers the most productive in Africa. UCDA runs around 1,000 nurseries and is expecting to distribute 30m plantlets to farmers this year.

'Government support has really helped, because we had reached a bottleneck. With coffee prices so miserable, the farmers cannot afford to buy new plants. But they will take the plants if they are free,' says William Naggaga of the UCDA.[101] The ICO and the Common Fund for Commodities have also been involved in projects to help farmers with pest control, a huge problem that hits incomes at a time when they are already on the floor.

Likewise, some companies have provided funds to help improve quality. Procter & Gamble's $1.5m grant to TechnoServe and the $500,000 grant to Oxfam America from Starbucks and the Ford Foundation are both focused on helping farmers improve the quality of the coffee they produce. For farmers benefiting from such schemes the advantages are considerable, but one-off initiatives of corporate philanthropy are not enough to tackle the scale of the crisis.

Raise prices, revive livelihoods

Roaster companies could commit to paying prices that provide farmers with a decent income, and manage their supply chains so as to ensure that farmers capture more of the benefits of the market and earn a decent income. That would be an income that more than covers the costs of production – leaving families capable of covering their needs in food, basic education, healthcare, and shelter. Calculations of such costs already exist – compiled both by coffee authorities in producer countries and by companies themselves – though they differ from country to country.

There are difficulties in establishing these costs for small farmers, as many inputs on such farms are not monetised, and small farmers face very different cost structures to bigger estates. However, these difficulties should not be an excuse for inaction. In few other industries would it even be necessary to argue that suppliers' costs need to be covered – but in few other industries do companies have the luxury of a supplier base that will continue to produce at a loss year in, year out.

Even if prices rise, farmers will still be exposed to the risk of price fluctuations. To tackle this problem, a private sector group has been forged under the aegis of the World Bank, which seeks to help smallholder producers manage the problem of price volatility. The taskforce brings together insurance and financial institutions in both developed and developing countries, and is currently conducting pilot schemes in several countries. The idea is to provide farmers with market-based instruments to secure a minimum price for their coffee.

As part of this work, a survey was conducted in Nicaragua to evaluate demand for the service among producers. Results indicated that even when prices are very low, farmers see the value in paying a premium to secure a fair market price for their coffee in the near future. Thus, a farmer would pay an 'insurance premium' that would give him or her the right, but not the obligation, to sell their coffee at a set price.

Retain and build value-adding capacity

For farmers, one of the few ways of adding value is by processing the coffee so that its quality can be proven. Coffee that has been hulled or depulped attracts a better price, pound for pound, than do the unprocessed cherries. Small-scale investments in appropriate technologies can yield significant results for farmers.

In Colombia, for instance, the Colombian Coffee Federation has developed a portable motor-driven mechanical processor that removes the pulp of the arabica cherry. If this were made available to farmers throughout rural areas, it could add significant value to their produce. Of course, for farmers to reap the benefits of such investments, they need to be able to sell into a market that rewards improved quality. National governments and buyers (local and international) have an important responsibility in this respect.

At a national level, the challenge for producing countries to add value is considerable. It is a challenge that must be tackled with urgency, with the aim of increasing processing in those countries. Adding value,

though, is not about processing alone. Branding, marketing, forging new routes to market and new ways of getting to consumers – these are all part of the value-added process, of which producer countries need to capture a bigger portion.

Establish real alternatives for rural development

Donor support is needed for any producer country that has developed a workable plan to reduce coffee production and support the poorest farmers. Viet Nam, for instance, has recently spoken of the need to reduce production of some of its low-grade and loss-making robusta varieties. Such plans would need support for transition costs and diversification, with special emphasis on poor women.

More generally, diversification efforts away from coffee have to be viewed in the light of negative trends in other commodities. The international community's adoption of an integrated approach to commodities is well overdue.

Conclusion

The current operation of the coffee market is causing misery across the developing world. The problems this is causing poor farmers and poor countries can no longer be ignored. Enough is enough. The coffee market must be made to work for the poor as well as the rich.

The failures of previous efforts at intervention in the market must be understood and lessons learned. But so too must the lessons of the moment. Asking some of the poorest and most powerless people in the world to negotiate in an open market with some of the richest and most powerful results, unsurprisingly, in the rich getting richer and the poor getting poorer. Active participation by all players in the coffee trade is needed to reverse this situation.

The next year is critical. Coffee-producing governments have agreed a plan that aims to reduce supply by improving the quality of coffee traded. This will only work if it is backed by the companies and by rich countries and is complemented by measures to address long-term rural underdevelopment.

Recommendations – A Coffee Rescue Plan

A Coffee Rescue Plan is needed, to bring supply back in line with demand and to support rural development, so that farmers can earn a decent living from coffee. The plan needs to bring together the major players in coffee to overcome the current crisis and create a more stable market.

Within one year, and under the auspices of the ICO, the Rescue Plan should result in:

1. Roaster companies committing to pay a decent price to farmers.

2. Roaster companies trading only in coffee that meets the ICO's Quality Coffee Scheme standards.

3. The destruction of at least five million bags, as an immediate measure, to be funded by consumer governments and roaster companies.

4. The creation of a Diversification Fund to help low productivity farmers create alternative livelihoods.

5. Roaster companies committing to buy increasing volumes of coffee under Fair Trade conditions directly from producers. Within one year this should apply to two per cent of their total volume, with subsequent incremental increases.

The Rescue Plan should be a pilot for a longer-term Commodity Management Initiative to improve commodity prices and provide alternative livelihoods for farmers. The outcomes should include:

1. Producer and consumer country governments establishing mechanisms to correct the imbalance in supply and demand to ensure reasonable prices to producers. Farmers should be adequately represented in such schemes.

2. Co-operation between producer governments to stop more commodities from entering the market than can be sold.

3. Support for producer countries to capture more of the value in their commodity products.

4. Extensive financing from donors to reduce small farmers' overwhelming dependence on agricultural commodities.

5. An end to EU and US double standards on agricultural trade that squeeze developing countries into a narrow range of options.

6. Companies paying a decent price for commodities (above the costs of production).

The Coffee Rescue Plan will only succeed if all participants in the coffee market are actively involved. The following recommendations include elements of what each group can do to make it work.

Coffee Companies

Roaster companies – Kraft, Nestlé, Procter & Gamble, and Sara Lee

1. Commit to paying a decent price to farmers.

2. Commit significant resources to tackle the coffee crisis (including a financial contribution to aid packages that deal with the crisis).

3. Label coffee products on the basis of their quality.

4. Commit to buying increasing volumes of coffee under Fair Trade conditions directly from producers. Within one year this should apply to two per cent of their total volume, with significant subsequent incremental increases to be determined annually by the Fair Trade movement.

5 Lobby the US government to rejoin the ICO.

6. Adopt clear and independently verifiable commitments to respect the rights of migrant and seasonal workers, including respect for ILO conventions.

Coffee retailers (supermarkets and coffee bars)

1. Demand of suppliers that the coffee they sell pays producers a decent price.

2. Promote Fair Trade coffee brands and products.

3. Insist that coffee products are labelled on the basis of their quality.

4. Starbucks to make public the findings of the commercial viability of its sourcing guidelines.

Governments and Institutions

International Coffee Organisation

1. Organise, with the UN and the participation of the World Bank, a high-level conference on the coffee crisis by February/March 2003, headed by Kofi Annan, specifying that participation is conditional on being willing and able to make concrete commitments.

2. Work with producer countries, Fair Trade organisations, and roaster companies to define a decent income for producers.

3. Implement the quality scheme, preceded by an impact assessment on small farmers.

World Bank

1. Identify World Bank support for producer countries to manage the short-term impact of coffee-price collapse, including rural development considerations in the Poverty Reduction Strategy Paper (PRSP) exercise. The World Bank and IMF should develop a long-term integrated strategy to tackle the problem of commodities.

2. Continue to review the HIPC process in light of the expected shortfall in export revenues resulting from the fall in commodity prices, and ensure that any country which suffers from a significant decline in commodity prices between Decision and Completion Point under HIPC automatically receives additional debt relief at Completion Point to ensure that it meets the 150 per cent debt-to-export target.

3. Contribute to a major international conference on coffee organised by the United Nations (UNCTAD) and the ICO by February/March 2003.

UN Conference on Trade and Development (UNCTAD)

1. Develop a long-term integrated strategy to tackle the problem of commodities.

2. Organise a major international conference on coffee with the ICO by February/March 2003.

Producer governments

1. Co-operate with each other to stop more commodities from entering the market than can be sold.

2. Put the issue of diversification at the centre of poverty-reduction strategies.

3. Provide support to farmers who have to leave the coffee market, including attention to women left on family farms.

4. Address the immediate needs of rural farmers for extension services including:

   • Technical and marketing information

   • Credit schemes and debt management services

These extension services should pay particular attention to the needs of women farmers.

5. Institute sanctions against anti-competitive trading practices that hurt small farmers.

6. Assess the impact of the ICO Quality Scheme on small producers, especially women farmers.

7. Protect the rights of seasonal and plantation workers to ensure that labour legislation, consistent with core

ILO conventions, is enacted and implemented. Particular attention should be paid to the rights of women labourers.

8. Promote small-producer associations and enterprises to strengthen poor farmers in national coffee markets.

Consumer governments

1. Provide political and financial support to tackle oversupply, including:

   - Support and financial help for the ICO Quality Scheme, including monitoring the quality of coffee entering their markets from each producer nation, and rapidly make this information public

   - Removal of remaining tariffs

   - Destruction of the lowest-quality coffee stocks

2. Support the ICO as the forum where producers and consumers can tackle the coffee crisis.

3. Increase funding for rural development and livelihoods in Overseas Development Assistance.

4. Provide incentives for roaster companies to undertake technology transfers and to carry out more of the value-added processing in developing countries.

Consumers

1. Buy more Fair Trade coffee.

2. Ask retailers to stock more Fair Trade products.

3. Demand that companies adopt pricing policies that guarantee a decent income to farmers.

4. Request better labelling on the origin of coffee from roasters/retailers.

5. Request that pension fund managers raise the questions below.

Investors

1. Encourage roaster companies to adopt supply-chain management schemes and pricing policies that pay above the costs of production and protect the labour rights of coffee workers, in the interests of the long-term sustainability of the coffee market.

2. Express the view to coffee companies in which they invest that improvements in the lives of poor farmers will be the criteria applied when assessing reputation risk management on issues of price and supply-chain management.

Notes

1 Deutsche Bank analyst report, 'Soluble Coffee: A Pot of Gold', 2 May 2000

2 Oxfam background research in Uganda, February 2002

3 'Bitter Coffee: How the Poor are Paying for the Slump in Coffee Prices', May 2001, Oxford: Oxfam (available in English and Spanish)

4 Source: FAO, ICO and World Bank 1997-98

5 Oxford Analytica Latin America Daily Brief, 19 June 2002

6 Oxfam background research in Brazil, February 2002

7 Business India, May 2002

8 Oxfam background research in Dak Lak province, April 2002, and research by ICARD

9 Interviews collected by Oxfam America, May 2002

10 Dow Jones newswires 29 May 2001

11 Oxfam background research in Ethiopia, April 2002

12 Dow Jones: 'Lower Coffee Prices, Drought Leave 30,000 Hondurans Hungry', 25 March 2002

13 Oxford Analytica, Daily Brief, 'Central America – The Coffee Crisis', 19 June 2002

14 Oxfam background research in Uganda, February 2002

15 Statement from the Integrated Regional Information Network (IRIN) UN Nairobi, 23 January 2002

16 'The Coffee Market: A Background Study', 2001, Oxford: Oxfam

17 'The Coffee Crisis in Perspective', Panos Varangis and Bryan Lewin, World Bank, 9 March 2002

18 Oxford Analytica, Latin America Daily Brief, 19 June 2002

19 Business India, May 2002

20 Name changed to protect identity

21 'Managing the Competitive Transition of the Coffee Sector in Central America', a discussion document by USAID, World Bank, and IADB, prepared for the regional workshop on the coffee crisis and its impact in Central America, Antigua, Guatemala, 3-5 April 2002

22 From 1999/00 to 2000/01 according to the ICO

23 Ugandan Coffee Development Authority, quoted by AFP wire agency on 10 June 2002, from Kampala, Uganda.

24 From 1999/00 to 2000/01, according to the ICO

25 World Bank data

26 Comments drawn from interviews and statements during the 3-5 April Central America coffee conference, held by the IADB, World Bank and USAID

27 Commodity exchange website, Government Aid Factsheet, updated 15 January 2002

28 Ibid

29 Ibid

30 Data given for crop years; last year refers to 2000/01

31 FO Licht: Estimate of World Coffee Production

32 Association of Coffee Producing Countries and Oxford Analytica

33 'Bumper Brazilian crop prompts fear of glut', Financial Times, 7 June 2002

34 This will feature in Brazil's production figures for the crop year 2002/03

35 Interview with Oxfam, Spring 2002

36 Economic Research Service USDA, Agricultural Outlook, March 1999

37 Data from the International Coffee Organization, expressed in nominal terms

38 These ratios adjust the green bean price for loss of weight so as to render this price comparable to the retail price

39 Oxfam background research in Peru, February 2002

40 This research was done by commodities economist and consultant Karen St Jean Kufuor

41 'Sustainable Coffee Survey of the North American Speciality Industry', Daniele Giovannucci, June 2001

42 Deutsche Bank analyst report: 'Soluble Coffee: A Pot of Gold?', 2 May 2000

43 This profit is struck after operating costs such as marketing, salaries, and processing are deducted

44 Margins refer to operating profit margins (before interest and tax)

45 Financial results for the nine months to March 2002 of fiscal year 2002

46 Ibid.

47 Quoted in 'Who Gains When Commodities are De-commodified?' R. Fitter & R. Kaplinsky, IDS, 2001

48 'Raising Nestlé price target to SFr410', Morgan Stanley equity research on food producers, 12 February 2002

49 Notes given to Oxfam from Nestlé, 18 July 2002

50 'Coffee Markets in East Africa: Local Responses to Global Challenges or Global Responses to Local Challenges', Stefano Ponte, Centre for Development Research Working Paper 01.5 Copenhagen, September 2001

51 Interview with Oxfam in Cincinatti, 11 June 2002

52 Notes given to Oxfam from Nestlé, 18 July 2002

53 Natural: arabica coffee where the beans have been removed from the cherry by drying in the sun, followed by hulling. This can give a harsher taste than that of washed coffee, where the cherry is de-pulped and the bean fermented before hulling.

54 'Managing the Competitive Transition of the Coffee Sector in Central America', a discussion document by USAID, World Bank, and IADB, prepared for the regional workshop on the coffee crisis and its impact in Central America, Antigua, Guatemala, 3-5 April 2002

55 'The Coffee Crisis in Perspective', Panos Varangis and Bryan Lewin, World Bank, 9 March 2002

56 'Germany, Market Strength', Bernhard Benecke, Coffee and Coca International, June 2000

57 Oxfam background research in Uganda, February 2002

58 Kraft Foods Third World Engagement, 'Presentation of Activities in Three Different Countries', document given to Oxfam at meeting on 8 April 2002

59 Ibid.

60 FO Licht International Coffee Report, 18 April 2002, 'Market Overview', by Peter Buzzanell

61 Graphs from the ACPC

62 'Managing the Competitive Transition of the Coffee Sector in Central America', a discussion document by USAID, World Bank, and IADB, prepared for the regional workshop on the coffee crisis and its impact in Central America, Antigua, Guatemala, 3-5 April 2002

63 FO Licht International Coffee Report, April 18, 2002. Market Overview by Peter Buzzanell

64 'Natural Enemies, Natural Allies', P.S. Baker, J. Jackson, S. Murphy

65 World Bank coffee presentation for the Coffee Association, 2002

66 Oxfam background research in Ethiopia, April 2002

67 'Dealing with Commodity Price Volatility in Developing Countries', International Task Force on Commodity Risk Management in Developing Countries, World Bank, 1999

68 'New World Bank Reports Confirm that the HIPC initiative is failing', Romilly Greenhill, Jubilee April 2002

69 ICO data

70 FAO Consultation, 'Back to Office Report by World Bank Officials', March 2002

71 Tea and Coffee Trade Journal, December 2001

72 Figures provided by the European Coffee Federation. The EU has recently allowed a quota for instant coffee with a 0 per cent rate up to a maximum volume. Brazil benefits from a large proportion of this quota allowance.

73 'Coffee Markets in East Africa: Local Responses to Global Challenges or Global Responses to Local Challenges', Stefano Ponte, Centre for Development Research Working Paper 01.5 Copenhagen, September 2001

74 Oxfam background research in Peru, February 2002

75 'Coffee Markets in East Africa: Local Responses to Global Challenges or Global Responses to Local Challenges', Stefano Ponte, Centre for Development Research Working Paper 01.5 Copenhagen, September 2001

76 'Quality, Marketing Structure and Farmer Remuneration in Cocoa and Coffee', seminar paper, Christopher Gilbert, ESI & FEWEB, Vrije Universiteit, Amsterdam, April 2002

77 Ibid.

78 Oxfam background research in Honduras, March 2002

79 Oxfam background research in Ethiopia, April 2002

80 Oxfam interviews in Dak Lak, Buonson and CuMgar provinces, May 2002

81 Oxfam background research in Peru, February 2002

82 Oxfam background research in Ethiopia, April 2002

83 Interviews collected by Oxfam America during the SCAA conference, May 2002

84 'Aid To Agriculture', OECD, December 2001
http://www.oecd.org/pdf/M00029000/M00029854.pdf

85 IFAD statement at International Conference on Financing for Development, Mexico, March 2002 (IFAD website)

86 'Rigged Rules and Double Standards: Trade, Globalisation, and the Fight Against Poverty', April 2002, Oxford: Oxfam

87 Ibid

88 'An Oversupply of Coffee Beans Deepens Latin America's woes', Peter Fritsch, Wall Street Journal, 8 July 2002

89 'Connoisseurs Lift Coffees to Vintage Status', Adrienne Roberts and Andrew Bounds, Financial Times, 5 July 2002

90 Agreed price established by FLO

91 NRI/DFID study on Fair Trade

92 Kraft Foods and Third World Engagement

93 Figure supplied by FLO based on volumes sold under labels

94 DataMonitor figures, March 2002

95 This is part of the Development Prospects work carried out by the World Bank. See http://www.worldbank.org/prospects/indexold.htm

96 'The Enhanced HIPC Initiative and the Achievement of Long-term External Debt Sustainability', World Bank paper for the Spring meetings, 2002

97 'Burundi Transitional Support Strategy', World Bank, February 2002

98 'Burundi: An interim strategy 1999–2001', World Bank, July 1999

99 'Interim Poverty Reduction Strategy Paper', IMF and IDA Joint Staff Assessment, January 2001

100 'Low Coffee Prices: Causes and Potential Solutions', Nestlé presentation to the CSR Europe, 12 July 2002

101 'The Coffee Crisis in Perspective', Panos Varangis and Bryan Lewin, World Bank, 9 March 2002

102 Based on modelling by Prof. Christopher Gilbert, which assumes a 2 cents/lb rise in the ICO composite price for every one million bags removed. Analysis conducted in 2001. Oxfam figures based on cost of removing very low quality beans at 15 cents/lb. Increase in export revenues, using ICO data, based on 2000/01 green bean exports of 84.189 million bags, and an average ICO composite price of 47.84 cents/lb, giving green bean export revenues during 2000/01 of $5,314m. Oxfam assumes export volumes stay constant in 2001/02, but subtracts the 5m bags to be removed. This would give total green bean volumes to be exported of 79.189 million bags at a new improved price of 57.84 cents/lb, yielding green bean exports worth $6,043m in export revenues. The benefit would be somewhat higher if one includes in the export totals the 5m bags of processed coffee from producing countries.

103 Oxfam background research in Uganda, February 2002

Background research

Casasbuenas, C. (2002) 'Coffee in Honduras: Crisis or Opportunity?'

Crabtree, J. (2002) 'Interviews with Coffee Farmers in Peru' (in Spanish) and 'Interviews with Coffee Industry Figures in Peru' (in English)

ICARD (2002) 'Impacts of Trade Liberalisation on Coffee Farmers in Dak Lak Province' (available later in 2002 from the Ministry of Agriculture and Rural Development in Viet Nam)

INESA (2001) 'Le Café en Haiti: Situation Actuelle at Plaidoyer pour une Amélioration de la Situation Socio-economique des Producteurs' (available in English and French)

Jean-Kufuor, K.S. (2002) 'Coffee Value Chain'

Knight, P. (2002) 'Interviews with Coffee Industry Figures in Brazil'

Mayne, R. (2002) 'The Coffee Crisis in Kafa Province of Ethiopia',

Oxfam (2001) 'The Coffee Market: A Background Study'

Oxfam (2001) 'Bitter Coffee: How the Poor are Paying for the Slump in Coffee Prices' (available in English and Spanish)

Pérez-Grovas, V., E. Cervantes and J. Burstein (2001) 'Case Study of the Coffee Sector in Mexico', Oxford: Oxfam

Sayer, G. (2002) 'Coffee Futures: The Impact of Falling World Prices on Farmers, Millers and Exporters in Uganda', Oxford: Oxfam

Oxfam's programme with coffee producers

Oxfam provides over $1.6m of support annually to a range of development programmes in coffee-producing regions – in Central America, Mexico, and the Caribbean, in South America, the Horn and East Africa, and East Asia. These programmes seek to strengthen the position of poorer coffee farmers in the market by increasing their business and technical skills and supporting their research, advocacy and campaigning. They also include help to small farmers to diversify out of coffee, and to enhance the quality of their coffee.

Oxfam works in partnership with the Fair Trade movement, which has brought significant benefits to poor coffee farmers around the world. Oxfam has supported Fair Trade networks that have developed in several regions with the aim of empowering producers and addressing the wider trade-policy agenda.

Oxfam International is a confederation of twelve development agencies that work in 120 countries throughout the developing world: Oxfam America, Oxfam-in-Belgium, Oxfam Canada, Oxfam Community Aid Abroad (Australia), Oxfam GB, Oxfam Hong Kong, Intermón Oxfam (Spain), Oxfam Ireland, Novib Oxfam Netherlands, Oxfam New Zealand, Oxfam Quebec, and Oxfam Germany. Please call or write to any of the agencies for further information.

Oxfam America
26 West St.
Boston, MA 02111-1206, USA
Tel: 1.617.482.1211
E-mail: info@oxfamamerica.org
www.oxfamamerica.org

Oxfam Canada
Suite 300, 294 Albert St.
Ottawa, Ontario, Canada K1P 6E6
Tel: 1.613.237.5236
E-mail: enquire@oxfam.ca
www.oxfam.ca

Oxfam Québec
2330 rue Notre-Dame Ouest
Bureau 200, Montréal, Québec
Canada H3J 2Y2
Tel: 1.514.937.1614
E-mail: info@oxfam.qc.ca
www.oxfam.qc.ca

Oxfam Ireland
Dublin Office:
9 Burgh Quay, Dublin 2, Republic of Ireland
Tel: 353.1.672.7662
E-mail: oxireland@oxfam.ie
Belfast Office:
52-54 Dublin Road, Belfast, BT2 7HN, UK
Tel: 44.28.9023.0220
E-mail: oxfam@oxfamni.org.uk
www.oxfamireland.org

Oxfam GB
274 Banbury Road, Oxford, OX2 7DZ, UK
Tel: 44.1865.311311
E-mail: oxfam@oxfam.org.uk
www.oxfam.org.uk

Oxfam-in-Belgium
Rue des Quatre Vents 60
1080 Brussels, Belgium
Tel: 32.2.501.6700
E-mail: oxfam@oxfam.be
www.oxfam.be

Novib Oxfam Netherlands
Mauritskade 9
2514 HD The Hague, The Netherlands
Postal address: P.O Box 30919, 2500 GX
The Hague, The Netherlands
Tel: 31.70.342.1621
E-mail: admin@novib.nl
www.novib.nl

Intermón Oxfam
Roger de Llúria 15
08010 Barcelona, Spain
Tel: 34.93.482.0700
E-mail: intermon@intermon.org
www.intermon.org

Oxfam Germany
Greifswalder Str. 33a
10405 Berlin, Germany
Tel: 49.30.428.50621
E-mail: info@oxfam.de
www.oxfam.de

Oxfam Hong Kong
17/F, China United Centre
28 Marble Road, North Point
Hong Kong
Tel: 852.2520.2525
E-Mail: info@oxfam.org.hk
www.oxfam.org.hk

Oxfam Community Aid Abroad
156 George St. (Corner Webb Street)
Fitzroy, Victoria, 3065 Australia
Tel: 61.3.9289.9444
E-mail: enquire@caa.org.au
www.caa.org.au

Oxfam New Zealand
Level 1, 62 Aitken Terrace
Kingsland, Auckland
New Zealand
Postal address: P.O. Box 68 357, Auckland 1032, New Zealand
Tel: 64.9.355.6500
E-mail: oxfam@oxfam.org.nz
www.oxfam.org.nz

Oxfam International Advocacy Offices

1112 16th Street, Suite 600, Washington, DC 20036, USA
Tel: 1.202.496.1170
E-mail: advocacy@oxfaminternational.org
www.oxfaminternational.org

Rue des Quatre Vents 60, 1080 Brussels, Belgium
Tel: 32.2.501.6761
E-mail: sonia.vila-hopkins@oxfaminternational.org

15 rue des Savoises
1205 Geneva
Tel: 41.22.321.2371
E-mail: celine.charveriat@oxfaminternational.org

355 Lexington Avenue, 3rd Floor, New York, NY10017, USA
Tel: 1.212.687.2091
E-mail: nicola.reindorp@oxfaminternational.org